LET ME TELL YOU
ABOUT
MY
GOD

THE PSALMS PORTRAY GOD

ROSALIE HAFFNER LEE

REVIEW AND HERALD PUBLISHING ASSOC
Washington, DC 20039-0555
Hagerstown, MD 21740

This book was
Edited by Gerald Wheeler
Designed by Richard Steadham
Cover by Howard Bullard

ISBN 0-8280-0215-0

R & H Cataloging Service
Bible. O.T. Psalms. English
    Let me tell you about my God! by Rosalie
Haffner Lee.

    1. Bible. O.T. Psalms—Commentaries.
I. Lee, Rosalie (Haffner), 1931-   II. Title.
        223.207

chp.-(X)

Contents

what is the psalm

pulling it all together

Dedication

In addition to expressing my gratitude to my husband, Ken, for his patience and encouragement during the time I worked on this manuscript, and to my parents, whose faith and confidence in me inspired me through the years, I would like to give credit to all my academy, college, and university Bible teachers who helped me develop a love for Bible study and taught me how to do it more effectively. But especially would I like to thank Arnold Wallenkampf (my college religion professor), who was responsible for my becoming involved in writing a quarter's Sabbath school lessons, and ultimately this book. His teaching and writing have inspired me through the years, and his confidence in me gave me the courage to attempt such a project.

"My mouth will tell of your righteousness,
  of your salvation all day long,
    though I know not its measure.
I will come and proclaim your mighty acts,
                O Sovereign Lord;
  I will proclaim your righteousness, yours alone. . . .
  Do not forsake, O God,
till I declare your power to the next generation,
  your might to all who are to come.
Your righteousness reaches to the skies, O God,
  you who have done great things.
  Who, O God, is like you?"

        Psalm 71:15-19, N.I.V.

Chapter 1

Let Me Tell You About My God

1- 18 - 62

A friend of mine carries in her purse a little book entitled *Let Me Tell You About My Grandchildren*. The slightest mention of her favorite subject is an invitation to share her prized album.

I carry a little book in my purse too. It contains some marvelous pictures of the greatest Person in the universe—portraits etched in words, ideas, and experiences. Some of the clearest and most beautiful revelations about my wonderful God emanate from the book of Psalms.

So, if you will—
"Come and listen, all you who fear God;
let me tell you" about my wonderful God:
"Great is the Lord and most worthy of praise."
Ps. 66:16; 145:3, N.I.V.

Christians in every age have read and loved the psalms—the poems, songs, and prayers of ancient Israel. Martin Luther suggested that they form a kind of miniature Bible, a microcosm of Scripture. Calvin referred to them as the anatomy of the soul, reflecting the "sorrows, troubles, fears, doubts, hopes, pains, perplexities, stormy outbreaks by which the hearts of men are tossed."

The psalms inspired Bach to write many of his great chorales. Isaac Watts wrote paraphrased hymns for each of the 150 psalms. The Huguenots sang the psalms set to melodies by some of the great Reformation composers, as did the Puritans on their way to America in search of religious freedom. The psalms have given birth to many of the great hymns of the Christian faith.

Why are the psalms so greatly loved? First of all, because they express the deepest needs and longings of the human heart. Someone has suggested that most of Scripture speaks *to* us, while the psalms speak *for* us. Like blank checks, we may read our own names and circumstances into them.

The psalms portray the greatness and majesty of Israel's God, while at the same time presenting Him as a personal, caring, and loving Father, listening to the cry of His children, responding to their needs, and answering their prayers. Pagan poets of Israel's time eulogized their gods, yet had to admit their remoteness and unconcern. But the psalmists tell of "my God," "my Shepherd," "my Rock." They could approach Him with their complaints, doubts, fears, and even their anger. And still trust in His great mercy and forgiveness.

The psalms, as part of a huge Old Testament mirror, reflect the life, suffering, and the glory of the coming Messiah (see Luke 24:27, 44-46). Jesus no doubt memorized many of the psalms at His mother's knee. He met temptation and rebuff with the songs He Himself had inspired through the Holy Spirit (see *Education*, p. 166). Our Saviour quoted from them more often than almost any other book of Scripture. Much of His teaching, such as the Sermon on the Mount, came from the psalms. (For an example, cf. Matt. 5:5 and Ps. 37:11.) Finally, He died with the words of Psalm 31:5 on His lips.

Unfortunately, some people think of the book of Psalms only as a collection of devotional prayers, interspersed with a lot of unlovely lashings-out at unidentified enemies. (We will consider the latter in chapters 8 and 10.) A speaker, challenging his audience to deeper Bible study, remarked that we need to graduate from a diet of devotional psalms to the "heavier meat" of the Word. But "meat" as heavy as you can take it lies hidden beneath their surface. And we may find the gospel of grace in their rich veins as surely as in the New Testament. In fact, Luther referred to certain psalms as being "Pauline" (see chapter 5).

So, the psalms with their varied moods, their wide range of subject matter, and their diversity of style form a mosaic of revealed truth about God—and about human life. In the following pages the author seeks to share a brief glimpse of some of the beauty, the richness, and the luster of that grand mosaic.

Do the psalms have relevance to God's people living in the last days of earth's history? Do they have significance to the great prophetic message Seventh-day Adventists have been called to give to the world?

Yes, for in their grand and complex designs we may trace the broad outlines of the great struggle between good and evil. How dare we preach Revelation 13 without the assuring promises of Psalm 91? And Psalm 46 is the perfect counterpart for Revelation 12. Luther once observed that not only is the book of Psalms a volume for times of trouble, but those being persecuted can best understand it. So the book of Psalms should stand with the great prophetic messages of Daniel and Revelation as crucial for a people living on the very knife-edge of time. "Amidst the deepening shadows of earth's last great crisis, God's light will shine brightest, and the song of hope and trust will be heard."—*Education*, p. 166.

Because this mosaic of truth is so broad yet so intricate, so rich yet so simple, writing a book about the Psalms reminds me of a 5-year-old child trying to scoop

9

up the Pacific with an eight-ounce cup. He doesn't make a dent in the ocean, but he certainly enjoys getting soaking wet in the process of trying.

God's greatness, His mercy, and His steadfast love transcend measure—our cups are too small. But we can delight in immersing ourselves in getting to know Him better. And what more inspiring way than to revel in some of the greatest literature ever written—the Psalms?

In order to do this, it is helpful to know something about their literary background.

WHAT IS A PSALM? Our English word *psalm* comes from the Greek term *psalmos,* a word referring to a song to be sung to the accompaniment of musical or stringed instruments. The Hebrew title of the Psalter, *Tehillim,* derives from the root word *halal* (from which we get our English word *hallelujah*). *Tehellim* means praises. Such lyric poems, intended to be sung, formed ancient Israel's hymnbook.

THE POETRY OF THE BIBLE. God loves beauty. Design and artistic loveliness marks all His creation, from the tiniest snowflake to the most magnificent heavenly bodies. Poetry is an art form breathed into throbbing human hearts by the Creator Himself.

The books of Job, Proverbs, Song of Solomon, Lamentations, as well as large portions of many of the prophets written in poetic style, comprise at least a fourth of the Old Testament writings.

A preacher, attacking some of the more modern translations of the Bible, once bemoaned, "And . . . they have turned the book of Isaiah into poetry."—In Ronald Barclay Allen, *Praise! A Matter of Life and Breath,* p. 49. Of course, Isaiah himself composed the poetry.

In addition to whole books of poetry, we find many

songs and poems scattered throughout Scripture. The first recorded psalm is the song of victory that Miriam led after Israel's crossing of the Red Sea (see Exodus 15). Many of David's psalms appear throughout the historical narrative, such as his song of deliverance in 2 Samuel 22.

Poetry appeals to our senses and speaks to our emotions. It must be felt and experienced. The poet can achieve his objective in various ways. For instance, he can use word pictures created through figures of speech, symbols, images, a play on words and sounds. Hebrew writers enjoyed colorful figures of speech: Ezekiel's dry bones, Amos' basket of summer fruit, Hosea's backsliding heifer, et cetera. A classic example found in the Psalms describes a bountiful harvest by such vivid word pictures as "thy paths drop fatness," "the pastures are clothed with flocks," and the valleys "shout for joy" (Ps. 65:11-13).

Hebrew poets expressed strong emotion through gross exaggeration. David has the cedars of Lebanon skipping like calves (Ps. 29:5, 6), the floods clapping their hands (Ps. 98:8). And he has God asking a rather ludicrous question, "Will I eat the flesh of bulls, or drink the blood of goats?" (Ps. 50:13). Understanding such dramatic use of images helps us to keep in proper perspective some of the psalmists' seeming strong statements, such as their violent outbursts against their enemies (see chapter 10 for examples).

Western poetic form, especially that of the English language, depends largely on rhyme and meter for poetic effect. But both the measured beat and the matching of sounds translate poorly from one language to another, often destroying the literary beauty in the process.

Hebrew poetry, on the other hand, uses a method known as parallelism as its main poetic element. Providentially, it lends itself to translation without as much loss of meaning or beauty. In 1928 scholars discovered an ancient Canaanite language in northern Syria that employed the same type of poetry as that found in the Bible. The Ugaritic tablets have thrown much light on our understanding of the psalms. Since then, some of the newer translations of the Bible have set the psalms into poetic form, according to the original intent.

Some have compared parallelism to stereophonic music. Two speakers instead of one give the music a "living" sensation of sound. So the Hebrew poets used repetition of ideas to achieve balance and poetic style (*ibid.*, p. 51).

Parallelism takes many forms, but a few examples of the main types will serve to illustrate the method:

In synonymous parallelism, the second line repeats the same idea as the first, but in different terms:

"Why standest thou afar off, O Lord?
why hidest thou thyself in times of trouble?" Ps. 10:1.

"Lord, who shall abide in thy tabernacle?
who shall dwell in thy holy hill?" Ps. 15:1.

However, in antithetical parallelism, one idea contrasts another:

"For the Lord knoweth the way of the righteous:
but the way of the ungodly shall perish." Ps. 1:6.

"With the pure thou wilt shew thyself pure;
and with the froward thou wilt shew thyself froward." Ps. 18:26.

Synthetic parallelism has the second line of the couplet develop or complete the thought of the first:

"I waited patiently for the Lord;
and he inclined unto me, and heard my cry." Ps. 40:1.

"I will both lay me down in peace, and sleep:
for thou, Lord, only makest me dwell in safety." Ps. 4:8.

THE SWEET SINGER OF ISRAEL. The psalms naturally make us think of David, though he did not author all of them. Scholars generally agree that the seventy-three psalms bearing his name, along with others that do not list an author, originated with him. (The apostles, for example, ascribe Psalm 2, though it is anonymous, to him in Acts 4:25.) Twelve of the psalms bear the name Asaph, a Levite and one of David's choir leaders. Eleven are attributed to the Sons of Korah. Psalm 90, titled "A Prayer of Moses," undoubtedly came from the Exodus leader's hand. Other authors include Heman, Ethan, and Jeduthun. But David stands out as a composer and collector of the psalms, and for making them a part of Israel's worship.

With a poet's heart and a musician's ear, he wrote songs that would "in all coming ages . . . kindle love and faith in the hearts of God's people, bringing them nearer to the ever-loving heart of Him in whom all His creatures live" (*Patriarchs and Prophets*, p. 642).

His musical career began early as a shepherd lad grazing his flocks on the Judean hillsides, where a thousand years later heavenly angels would announce the Saviour's birth to other shepherds watching their flocks at night. In the solitude of the fields "the rich melody of his voice poured out upon the air" in sweet anthems of devotion and adoration (*ibid.*).

Later, as King Saul's minstrel he charmed away depression with the soothing strains of his harp. When driven from the court by the insanely jealous Saul, he learned to take refuge in the "shadow of thy wings" (Ps. 57:1). Some of his most poignant songs he composed during this period of his life (see *Patriarchs and Prophets*, pp. 658, 664).

As Israel's king, he experienced the heights of joy that inspired some of the most exalted hymns of worship. He also tasted the bitterness of guilt and remorse, resulting in the penitential psalms, which have blessed and comforted God's children through the centuries.

"The psalms of David pass through the whole range of experience, from the depths of conscious guilt and self-condemnation to the loftiest faith and the most exalted communing with God. . . . Of all the assurances which His word contains, it is one of the strongest testimonies to the faithfulness, the justice, and the covenant mercy of God."—*Ibid.*, p. 754.

It is helpful to reread the story of David's life when studying the psalms. Get to know the "man who was raised up on high, the anointed of the God of Jacob, and the sweet psalmist of Israel" (2 Sam. 23:1). As surely as "the Spirit of the Lord spake by me, and his word was in my tongue" (verse 2), so surely his songs will speak to us and their message will be on our tongues and in our hearts.

King David as a musician did much to organize and promote the worship of God through sacred music. Not only was he responsible for writing and collecting the psalms and giving ancient Israel their hymnbook, but also he organized the music and liturgy of their worship (see 1 Chronicles 23 through 29). David composed special psalms for specific occasions, such as Psalm 24 for the transfer of the ark to Jerusalem (see 2 Sam. 6:12). In addition, he designed musical instruments for divine worship (1 Chron. 23:5; Amos 6:5).

The superscriptions of many of the psalms, phrases like *sheminith, gittith, mahalath,* probably had musical significance, comparable to our *crescendo, animato, legato,* et cetera. Other terms such as *neginoth* may have indicated what musical instruments should accompany the psalm. The expression *selah,* of uncertain meaning, appears seventy-one times in the Psalter, and probably had some musical significance.

The Psalter contains five collections of psalms, each ending with a doxology. Book One includes Psalms 1-41 and closes with a double Amen. Book Two consists of Psalms 42-72 and concludes with the inscription "The prayers of David the son of Jesse are ended." (The psalms of David, though, appear in all of the books.) Book Three embraces Psalms 73-89, and Book Four, Psalms 90-106. Book Five, Psalms 107-150, comprises the songs of ascent or pilgrim songs (Psalms 120-134) and many of the great hallel (praise) hymns such as Psalms 111-117, 135, 146-150.

Just how the various divisions came about is not entirely clear. The Israelites may have collected them as individual hymnbooks, and later combined them into one psalter. Some students of the Psalms see in the five books a significant parallel to the five books of the Pentateuch (the Books of Moses). Certainly, the psalms reflect Israel's theology, history, and worship as revealed in the Pentateuch.

TYPES OF PSALMS. Among the great hymns of praise are the nature psalms, the royal or coronation hymns, the historical narratives and the national or Zion songs, the praise and thanksgiving hymns, wisdom psalms (written in a teaching style), and the pilgrim songs. But by far the largest number of the psalms fall into the category of prayers and laments, some of the community, others of the individual petitioner. A lament is a cry of distress from someone in trouble, appealing to God for aid, sometimes making a confession of guilt or innocence. Usually it includes an expression of confidence in God's ability and willingness to help. Finally, it contains a pledge or vow of gratitude and praise in return. (For further information on the classification of the

Psalms, see *The SDA Bible Commentary*, vol. 3, pp. 623-625.)

Martin Luther believed that the psalms were a kind of school of prayer where "the Christian can learn to pray . . . for here he can hear how the saints talk with God."

Dietrich Bonhoeffer, a German theologian who eventually became a martyr for his faith at the hands of the Nazi regime, studied Luther's translation of the Psalms, and held with him that they represent the prayer book of the Bible where we may learn to pray God's words. Such prayers, he said, may not necessarily represent our feelings or desires at any given moment, but if we would pray aright, we must learn to pray God's words, not just our own. "The richness of the Word of God ought to determine our prayer, not the poverty of our heart."— *Psalms: The Prayer Book of the Bible*, p. 15.

HOW TO GET THE MOST FROM YOUR STUDY OF THE PSALMS. Pray the psalms. Sing them. Memorize them. And study them. Keep a notebook handy as you study. Begin by making an outline for each psalm. Read them in some of the newer Bible translations, such as *The New International Version*, the *New American Standard Bible*, and *The Jerusalem Bible*. (The book of Psalms in the latter translation is available by itself.) Use *The SDA Bible Commentary* and other good commentaries on the Psalms.

Years ago when I first began a serious study of the Psalms I made notations of certain key words and phrases especially meaningful to me. For example, one column contained all the references in the Psalms using the words *salvation* and *save*. (There are at least 130 such verses.)

Make your own list of psalms for special circumstances. Read Psalms 3 and 4, for example, when you are troubled and can't sleep.

Copy some of your favorite excerpts onto cards and carry them in a small pocket notebook. You may memorize while you walk, while you work, and when you travel. Meditate as you memorize. Thus you will be making those wonderful prayers and songs your own.

"There are few means more effective for fixing His words in the memory than repeating them in song. And such song has wonderful power. It has power to subdue rude and uncultivated natures; power to quicken thought and to awaken sympathy, to promote harmony of action, and to banish gloom and foreboding that destroy courage and weaken effort. . . . It [song] is one of the most effective means of impressing the heart with spiritual truth."—*Education*, pp. 167, 168.

Make the prayers and songs of the Psalter your daily companions. Let them bless your home and your own heart with their message of the infinite greatness and the ever-abiding presence of our wonderful God. Heaven can begin here as you learn its keynote of praise through the Psalms.

"The Psalms were meant for all time. Other things grow old, but these do not. Other things die, but these live. Cut across the arteries of their life anywhere, and they bleed. Songs which like the Psalms have stood the test of three thousand years may well be said to contain in them the seed of eternity."—Quoted in Charles Herbert Morgan, *The Psalms as Daily Companions*, pp. 9, 10.

Chapter 2

In Praise of the Creator

Let me tell you about my God: He is the Creator of the universe.

"By the word of the Lord were the heavens made;
and all the host of them by the breath of his mouth.

. . .

Let all the earth fear the Lord:
let all the inhabitants of the world stand in awe of
him.

For he spake, and it was done;
he commanded, and it stood fast." Ps. 33:6-9.

How much "organic soup" do you think it would take to bring together just the right amounts and types of chemicals for a simple protein to form by chance? Someone has suggested that the earth would have to be blanketed with a half-mile thickness of amino acids (the substances that make up protein) for a billion years just to provide opportunity for the spontaneous appearance of the simplest kind. A Swiss mathematician, Charles Guye, computed the odds against such chance formation as being 10^{160} to one.

I believe that a Master Designer planned and combined the right molecules into a living organism. And He brought it into existence by a Word. The same Word revealed Himself as a personal God in communication with the prophets of old. "Hear, O heavens, and give ear,

O earth: for the Lord hath spoken" (Isa. 1:2). "The word of the Lord came to me" (Jer. 2:1). And that "Word was made flesh, and dwelt among us" (John 1:14).

On March 19, 1981, Arkansas Governor Frank White signed into law Act 590, which required that the State's public schools give equal time to both creation science and evolutionary theory. The Civil Liberties Union contested the law, and the court hotly debated it before ruling it unconstitutional on January 5, 1982. The judge based his decision on his conclusion that "Creation-science presupposes a Creator to be the single most significant reason why it could not be classified as a science. Therefore . . . it must be religious and unconstitutional."—Quoted in "Report on Creation Trial," Ralph Blodgett, *Adventist Review,* Feb. 18, 1982, p. 7.

The scientists who testified in behalf of the prosecution virtually scoffed at Creation-science as "an absurd and completely disproven theory." Listening to the news coverage of the trial at the time we couldn't help sensing the scorn and ridicule with which even usually unbiased reporters treated the story. Such mockery is not new. The psalmist must have been familiar with it, for he wrote:

"Lord, how long shall the wicked,
how long shall the wicked triumph?
How long shall they utter and speak hard things?
and all the workers of iniquity boast themselves?

. . .

Understand, ye brutish among the people:
and ye fools, when will ye be wise?
He that planted the ear, shall he not hear?
he that formed the eye, shall he not see?" Ps. 94:3-9.

When was the last time you held a newborn baby in your arms and marveled at such an awesome bit of creation? Who designed those intricate little fingers so perfectly? Fingers that will someday form a man's strong hand or possess a woman's gentle touch? Who planned those complex little ears? Ears that can detect the eerie call of an owl or be mystified by the musical tones and harmony of Niagara Falls? Who formed those bright little eyes that over a lifetime will send millions of images to that tiny brain? A brain that defies the most complex man-made computer?

Science cannot explain the work of Creation and the mystery of life. "Through faith we understand that the worlds were framed by the word of God, so that things which are seen were not made of things which do appear" (Heb. 11:3).

Creation by divine fiat forms the very foundation pillar of Biblical faith. From Genesis to Revelation, His right to obedience and worship, His right to rule and to judge, and His right to save, all derive from and rest on His authority as Creator of the universe.

The well-known nature psalms praise the Creator, not the creation. Or as one writer so aptly put it, nature "speaks not of herself, but of her divine Originator. Nature leads all the psalmists into the courts of reverence and adoration of the Creator."—C. H. Morgan, *The Psalms as Daily Companions*, p. 41.

"God's handiwork in nature is not God Himself in nature. The things of nature are an expression of God's character. . . . It is not nature but the God of nature that is to be exalted."—*Testimonies*, vol. 8, p. 263.

"Know ye that the Lord he is God:
it is he that made us, and not we ourselves;
we are his people, and the sheep of his pasture."
"O come, let us worship and bow down:
let us kneel before the Lord our maker."
"For all the gods of the nations are idols:

but the Lord made the heavens." Ps. 100:3; 95:6; 96:5.

False theories of man's origin have degraded his God-given value and dignity. We shuddered when we heard that a madman in a small town not far from our own community had gunned down six people. But in a few days we'd all but forgotten, and barely winced at reports of hundreds of deaths in the Middle East. So while our society argues the legal implications of issues like abortion and euthanasia, it says in actions louder than words, "Life is cheap!"

The psalmist too lived in a society and in an age when life was cheap. But his contact with nature's God gave him deep insights into the worth of a human life.

MAN, THE CREATOR'S CROWNING WORK: PSALM 8. Picture the young David on a dark, lonely hillside, staring up into a star-studded sky. Overwhelmed with the vastness of the heavens and the brilliance of its jewels, he whispers in wonderment and awe:

"When I consider thy heavens, the work of thy fingers,
the moon and the stars, which thou hast ordained;
what is man, that thou art mindful of him?
and the son of man, that thou visitest him?" Verses 3, 4.

But God thought enough of him to create a being fearfully and wonderfully made (see Ps. 139:13-16). After providing him with a heart that beats an average of 100,800 times a day to move a total of twenty tons of blood (equal to the weight of 250 people); with a mind capable of designing satellites and spaceships and sending them to the moon to explore the mysteries of space; with senses to feel, to hear, to touch, to smell, and to see the wonders of God's creation—surely He must care for him!

"For thou hast made him a little lower than the
angels,

and hast crowned him with glory and honour."
Verse 5.

When asked his view of the origin of man, the famous
English author Thomas Carlyle declared, "Gentlemen,
you place man a little higher than the tadpole. I hold with
the ancient singer, 'Thou hast made him a little lower
than the angels.'"

Instead of slowly evolving from some lower form of
life, the being made in God's own image received
"dominion over the works of thy hands; thou hast put all
things under his feet" (verse 6).

The psalm speaks to the deepest need of the human
soul—that of identity. Who am I? Where did I come
from? Why am I here? Man, the crowning work of the
Creator, made to love, honor, and worship his Maker,
remains incomplete and unfulfilled until he answers to
the purpose of his creation. Here we begin to sense our
dignity and worth as human beings.

"All who live in communion with our Creator will
have an understanding of His design in their creation. . . .
They will seek neither to glorify nor to depreciate
themselves."—*Testimonies*, vol. 8, p. 63.

"The value of a soul, who can estimate? Would you
know its worth, go to Gethsemane."—*Christ's Object
Lessons*, p. 196.

With such an understanding of ourselves and our
wonderful God, we can say with the psalmist:

"O Lord, our Lord,

how excellent is thy name in all the earth!" Verse 9.

THE TWO BOOKS—NATURE AND REVELA-
TION: PSALM 19. During the French Revolution, Jean
Bon St. Andre threatened a peasant that he would "have

all your steeples pulled down, that you may no longer have any object by which you may be reminded of your old superstitions."

The humble peasant replied, "But you cannot help leaving us the stars!"—Charles H. Spurgeon, *Psalms*, on Ps. 19:1.

Men may ignore His Written Word, they may reject the Incarnate Word, but they cannot escape the testimony of the stars. Nature is a universal language that speaks to all who will listen.

"The heavens are telling the glory of God;
   and the firmament proclaims his handiwork." Ps.
   19:1 (from Artur Weiser, *The Psalms: A Commentary*).

Spurgeon once said that the "book of nature has three leaves, heaven, earth and sea. . . . He who begins to read creation by studying the stars begins the book at the right place."—*Op. cit.*, on Psalm 19.

The silence of nature speaks eloquently of God's wisdom and might. The laws of nature like those of His Written Word reveal an Infinite Mind behind the design and intricacy of every living thing.

"Day to day pours forth speech,
   and night to night whispers knowledge.
There is no language nor are there words
   in which their voice is not heard.
Their law is proclaimed throughout all the world,
   and their words go to the end of the earth." Verses
   2-4 (From Weiser, *op. cit.*).

Artur Weiser, a German student of the psalms, suggests that nature itself is a powerful record of creation, and for those who have eyes to see and ears to hear, every day is a new page in the record of the history of God's creative acts (*ibid.*, p. 198).

"He has set a tent in the sea for the sun

which comes forth like a bridegroom leaving his
chamber,
and like a strong man runs its course with joy."
Verses 4, 5 (from Weiser, *op. cit.*).

Nearly all of the ancients worshiped the sun. One of
their legends had it resting in the arms of his beloved—
the sea—at night, and arising in the morning in vigor and
radiant splendor. David may have borrowed the idea for
his poetic image, but he did so by way of contrast. It is not
the sun he glorifies, but its Creator. He sets Israel's God
apart from and above all other deities.

"For I know that the Lord is great,
and that our Lord is above all gods." Ps. 135:5.

The last half of Psalm 19 extols the virtues of God's
other book, His self-revelation in the Written Word or
the Law. (Law here, as in other psalms, encompasses all
of God's revealed will, not just the Ten Commandments
or Mosaic code.)

Spurgeon commented that as Aristotle had two types
of books, one for the common people, and the other for
his private scholars and close friends, so God has two
kinds—the book of nature for all mankind (verses 1-6)
"and the book of His Scriptures as a statute book for His
. . . church" (verses 7, 8). And "my Father wrote them
both."—*Op. cit.*, on Psalm 19.

"Nature and revelation alike testify of God's love."—
Steps to Christ, p. 9. As the physical creation reveals
beauty and order, so the written law is "sweeter also than
honey" and more valuable than "fine gold"; and just as the
heat of the sun penetrates everywhere, so the law reaches
the soul, revealing hidden sins and "secret faults" (verses
10, 12).

This great psalm, of which Derek Kidner has said, "Its
theology is as powerful as its poetry" (*Psalms 1-12: An
Introduction and Commentary*, p. 97), ends with an

eloquent prayer:
> "Let the words of my mouth, and the meditation of
> my heart,
> be acceptable in thy sight,
> O Lord, my strength, and my redeemer." Verse 14.

CREATOR AND SUSTAINER: PSALM 104. Psalm 104 stands among the giants of the praise psalms. Its vivid word pictures and the movement with which it describes the Creation week make it a literary masterpiece. Someone has suggested that it would be worth ten years of study to be able to read it in the original Hebrew (see *The SDA Bible Commentary,* vol. 3, p. 863).

The poem begins by describing God in regal splendor wrapping Himself in a robe of light (verse 2) (Day 1; cf. Gen. 1:3-5), then stretching out the heavens (firmament) and building His palace on the waters (gathering together of the waters, Day 2; cf. Gen. 1:6-8). He rides His chariot of clouds (His omnipresence) and sends forth His angel messengers like the wind to minister to His creatures.

The Lord waters the hills and makes the grass to grow for the cattle, and provides seed for man to cultivate for bread (verse 14) (Day 3; cf. Gen. 1:9-13; see also Ps. 104:5-9).

The Creator has set the heavenly bodies for seasons and for days (verse 19) (Day 4; cf. Gen. 1:14-19). The Author of all life provides homes for the birds of the air and for the fish of the sea (verses 16, 17, 25, 26) (Day 5; cf. Gen. 1:20-23), and supplies the needs of all His creatures, including man (verses 21-23) (Day 6; cf. Gen. 1:24-28).

> "Yahweh, what variety you have created,
> arranging everything so wisely!
>
> Earth is completely full of things you have
> made. . . .
> All creatures depend on you

to feed them throughout the year;
you provide the food they eat,
with generous hand you satisfy their hunger."
Verses 24-27, Jerusalem.

"From the solemn roll of the deep-toned thunder and old ocean's ceaseless roar, to the glad songs that make the forests vocal with melody, nature's ten thousand voices speak His praise. In earth and sea and sky, with their marvelous tint and color . . . we behold His glory. The everlasting hills tell us of His power. . . . The living green that carpets the brown earth tells of God's care for the humblest of His creatures. . . . All things tell of His tender, fatherly care and of His desire to make His children happy."—*The Ministry of Healing*, pp. 411, 412.

In 1715 Isaac Watts wrote a paraphrased hymn for children based on this psalm and the Creation story found in Genesis 1. That hymn, "I Sing the Mighty Power," has become a favorite praise song for all of God's children. Read its words again (*Church Hymnal*, No. 93) and see how closely it describes Creation week as portrayed in this psalm.

Overwhelmed with the greatness of his God, the psalmist feels he must share his testimony:
"I mean to sing to Yahweh all my life,
I mean to play for my God as long as I live.
May these reflections of mine give him pleasure,
as much as Yahweh gives me!" Verses 33, 34,
Jerusalem.

The psalm closes with a wish for sinners to vanish from the earth, a strange ending to such a beautiful nature psalm. Or is it? Have you ever wished some starlit night that you could just walk and walk and walk—alone—to enjoy the beauty and solitude? Then you remembered that sinners still wander in the land, and abandoned the impulse. Or when traveling along a scenic mountain pass have you suddenly come upon some "sinner's" litter—beer cans and all the rest?

No, the psalmist didn't go off on a tangent when he prayed for the elimination of sinners. Rather, he recognized them as the one discordant note in an otherwise harmonious universe. And he with other prophets looked forward to the time when "there shall be no more curse" (Rev. 22:3), when sin and sinners shall be so completely removed from the earth that "it shall leave them neither root nor branch" (Mal. 4:1). In that day when God shall "make all things new" (Rev. 21:5). Eden restored will once again ring with praises to the Creator and Sustainer of all living things.

A CALL TO WORSHIP.
"Praise ye the Lord.
Praise ye the Lord from the heavens:
praise him in the heights."
"Kings of the earth, and all the people;
princes, and all judges of the earth:
both young men, and maidens;
old men, and children:
let them praise the name of the Lord:
for his name alone is excellent;
his glory is above the earth and heaven." Ps.
148:1, 11-13.

God's last call to our planet is one to worship the Creator (Rev. 14:7). A large segment of the human family has set aside and ignores the memorial of His creative power, the sign of His authority (Ex. 31:17). But our Creator calls us to "remember the sabbath day, to keep it holy" (chap. 20:8). For it reminds us that "he is our God; and we are the people of his pasture" (Ps. 95:7), that we exist to worship "the Lord our Maker" (verse 6).

Let Me Tell You About My God

" 'The Sabbath therefore lies at the very foundation of divine worship.' "—*The Great Controversy*, p. 437.

Chapter 3

Great Is Thy Faithfulness

Let me tell you about my God—the covenant-keeping God, a God of mercy and faithfulness to His people Israel.
"I will sing of the mercies of the Lord for ever:
with my mouth will I make known thy faithfulness
to all generations." Ps. 89:1.
The story of His intention to save man, of His reaching into history in every generation to make contact with the rebellious race, is the account of a God who never gives up. We may summarize His overtures in one word—*covenant*.

A covenant is an agreement between two persons. God and Christ entered into a covenant to save the lost race as soon as the crisis of sin arose (see *The Desire of Ages*, p. 22). He made one with Noah to save as many as would respond to the call to enter the ark before a flood destroyed the world (Gen. 6:18). The Lord established a covenant with His friend Abraham (chap. 15:18) to produce from him a great nation—a people He hoped would tell the whole world how great it is to be in special family relationship to the God of the universe.

The story of Israel is the narrative of God's covenant mercy and lovingkindness, the history of salvation in operation. (That is why theologians often refer to Israel's history as salvation history.)

Their religion rested on the great historical milestones of their deliverance from Egyptian bondage, the giving of the law at Sinai, their wilderness wanderings, and finally their establishment in Canaan. Nowhere in Scripture do we find the events more profoundly presented than in Israel's national hymns, Psalms 78, 105, 106, and 107.

Why should we study them?

First of all, their study helps us to understand the entire Psalter better, for they give us insights into Israel's religious life and culture. Second, they present God's perspective of history, providing an interpretation or an explanation of Israel's experience in the light of divine revelation. Finally, the national hymns do have relevance to God's modern Israel. Ellen White urged "that these chapters be read at least once every week" by everyone, for they contain warnings for our day (*Testimonies to Ministers*, p. 98). "By carefully studying these scriptures we may be able to appreciate more fully the goodness, mercy, and love of our God."—*Testimonies*, vol. 8, p. 107.

"MAKE KNOWN HIS DEEDS": PSALM 105. Psalm 105 begins with a song of thanksgiving to God for His mighty deeds. Asaph and his fellow musicians sang at least part of the psalm on the occasion of the transfer of the ark of the covenant to the City of David (1 Chron. 16:1, 7-22). It is joyous and full of praise to God for His great faithfulness. Beginning with the covenant made to Abraham, it traces the history of God's chosen through to the Exodus and their entrance into the Promised Land.

"O give thanks unto the Lord; call upon his name:
make known his deeds among the people. . . .
Remember his marvellous works that he hath done;
his wonders, and the judgments of his mouth."
Verses 1-5.

God found in Abraham one willing to respond to the summons to enter into covenant relationship with Himself. Without any visible tokens of fulfillment, Abraham acted on God's promise, "I will make of thee a great nation" (Gen. 12:2).

"By faith Abraham, when he was called . . . , obeyed; and he went out, not knowing whither he went" (Heb. 11:8). Imagine how he must have agonized during the long years of waiting for the promised seed. Yet everywhere he went he set up his altar as a witness to his worship of the living God and his faith in Him.

And what thoughts must have coursed through Isaac's mind as he watched his favorite son, Esau, drift farther and farther away from his father's faith? As for Jacob, the old patriarch did not know whether he would ever see his son again. Then during Jacob's long life of twisted fate, of "evil" days (Gen. 47:9) and heartbreaking family trage- dies, how often must he have wondered how God would bring into existence His purposes.

But God "remembered his covenant. . . . Which covenant he made with Abraham, and his oath unto Isaac; and confirmed the same unto Jacob . . . , and to Israel for an everlasting covenant" (Ps. 105:8-10).

"He reproved kings for their sakes." (verse 14). "He sent a man . . . Joseph . . . whose feet they hurt with fetters" (verses 17, 18). "He increased his people greatly; and made them stronger than their enemies" (verse 24). Then "he sent Moses . . . and Aaron" (verse 26). And through them He "shewed . . . signs . . . and wonders" (verse 27) until "Egypt was glad when they departed" (verse 38). "He brought them forth . . . : and there was not one feeble person among their tribes" (verse 37).

Parents who have dreamed for their children, and then given and sacrificed everything they had to make those dreams come true, must know a little of how God felt when He had done so much for His people.

He "satisfied them with the bread of heaven" and "opened the rock, and the waters gushed out" (verses 40, 41). "For he remembered his holy promise. . . . And he brought forth his people with joy, and his chosen with gladness: and gave them the lands of the heathen: . . . that they might observe his statutes, and keep his laws" (verses 42-45). Loyalty, love, and obedience—the essence of a good relationship, the basis for the covenant—that's all He asked in return.

GOD'S PURPOSE FOR ISRAEL: PSALM 78. Psalm 78, the longest of the national hymns, might be titled "Lest We Forget!" It is much more than a rehearsal of events; it is a meditation on the history of God's people in the light of His saving deeds in their behalf. The psalm begins with an invitation to listen to the "dark sayings" or riddles "our fathers have told us"—how God's purposes and plans continue in spite of Israel's failures.

Such lessons they were to pass on "to the generation to come," because they indicated "his wonderful works that he hath done" (verse 4). God's people were to make known His testimony and law so "that they might set their hope in God, and not forget the works of God, but keep his commandments" (verse 7).

He had called Israel to be a "special people unto himself, above all people that are upon the face of the earth." However, He did not choose them because they "were more in number than any people," but because of His great love and for the sake of "the oath which he had sworn" to their fathers (Deut. 7:6-8).

The world and time in which Israel appeared on the scene contained many examples of corrupt peoples who had demonstrated the end results of defying divine laws. As the pagan nations filled up their cup of iniquity, God would drive them out and give their land to His covenant people. But He warned Israel not to take up the practices and sins for which others had fallen under judgment.

God's covenant people were to be Exhibit A of obedience to the perfect laws of an all-wise God. Their spirituality, their prosperity, their well-ordered families, and their wisdom and skill in every branch of learning would testify to the superiority of their religion and the sovereignty of their God.

Compliance to His laws would result in good health—freedom from the devastating diseases of the surrounding nations. Even the soil would respond to attention to His laws by producing more bountifully. Their animals would be healthier and more fertile (see verses 13, 14). Through their establishment in, and full occupation of, the Promised Land they would become missionaries to the whole world. Eventually, their kingdom would embrace the world (see *Christ's Object Lessons*, pp. 285-290).

ISRAEL'S FAILURE AND GOD'S FAITHFULNESS: PSALM 106. Psalm 106 begins with praise and thanksgiving to God for His goodness and enduring mercy.

"Who can utter the mighty acts of the Lord?
who can shew forth all his praise?" Verse 2.

God's favor to His people in ages past is the psalmist's personal assurance of salvation:

"We have sinned with our fathers,
we have committed iniquity, we have done wickedly. . . .
Nevertheless he saved them for his name's sake,
that he might make his mighty power to be known."
Verses 6-8.

We can sum up the story of Israel's failure and God's

faithfulness in a few words—*"they* soon *forgat"* "God their saviour," but *"he remembered* for them his covenant" (verses 13, 21, 45).

Hardly had they escaped the Egyptian armies at the Red Sea before they began murmuring for water, provoking Him who with mighty power had led them through (verses 7-9). Barely had the songs of praise for their deliverance wafted out over the desert air before they began lusting for the "flesh pots of Egypt" (verse 14).

Years before the writing of the psalm, Moses had described God's keen disappointment over Israel's forgetfulness:

"But Jeshurun waxed fat, and kicked: . . .
then he forsook God which made him,
and lightly esteemed the Rock of his salvation.
. . .
Of the Rock that begat thee thou art unmindful,
and hast forgotten God that formed thee." Deut.
32:15-18.

Did Israel suffer from amnesia? Was there something in their genes that made them forget so quickly? Or was their affliction the story of the conflict between the power of God and that of sin that rages in the hearts and lives of His people in every age?

What can we learn from looking at the tragic snapshots in the Psalms' photo album? What is the nature of the sin of forgetfulness that so persistently plagued them throughout their history?

Forgetfulness is deliberate disobedience (see Deut. 8:11). It is King Saul returning from the battle with cattle that should have been destroyed (1 Sam. 15:14, 15).

Forgetfulness is careless inattention or indifference to God's express will; it is Uzzah touching the ark (2 Sam. 6:7) or Nadab and Abihu offering strange fire (Lev. 10:1, 2).

Forgetfulness is placing the fear of man above that of God (Isa. 51:12, 13); it is Aaron casting a golden calf at Horeb (Ex. 32:21-24).

Forgetfulness is idolatry (Jer. 18:15; 23:27), Israel worshiping the molten image, changing "their glory into the similitude of an ox" (Ps. 106:19, 20). No wonder Moses had repeatedly warned, "Beware lest thou forget the Lord"; "Remember, and forget not"; "Hearken" (Deut. 6:12; 9:7; 30:10).

Forgetfulness is flaunting our unbelief before God. They "lusted exceedingly in the wilderness, and tempted God in the desert" (Ps. 106:14). "There is nothing at all, beside this manna" (Num. 11:6). "Can God furnish a table in the wilderness?" (Ps. 78:19). We don't like what You've put on the table! "Who shall give us flesh to eat?" (Num. 11:4). Respecting their power of choice, "he gave them their request; but sent leanness into their soul" (Ps. 106:15).

When the serpent came to Eve in the Garden, his first temptation was "Try it—you'll like it!" The appeal to satisfy the physical appetite brought about the fall of the human family. The pitiful results of Israel's lusting in the wilderness demonstrated the utter helplessness and hopelessness of man's ability to cope with his own fallen nature. "They were not estranged from their lust," even after God's wrath had slain the "fattest of them" (Ps. 78:30, 31).

But the redemption of the race and hope for man's restoration became sure in another wilderness when the Son of God refused to yield to the temptation to satisfy legitimate hunger. "Man shall not live by bread alone" (Matt. 4:4), He declared. "Temperance in all things has more to do with our restoration to Eden than men realize."—*Counsels on Diet and Foods*, p. 43.

The murmuring, complaining spirit that so frequently

afflicted Israel all too often had their leaders as its target. "They envied Moses . . . and Aaron the saint of the Lord" (Ps. 106:16). Korah, Moses' cousin, cherished pride and ambition, which bred envy and jealousy that eventually erupted into open rebellion, the same spirit that had caused the first rebellion in heaven.

Why did God deal so severely with Korah, Dathan, and Abiram? Because "it is hardly possible for men to offer greater insult to God than to despise and reject the instrumentalities He would use for their salvation."— *Patriarchs and Prophets,* p. 402.

Korah and his associates honestly believed they were in the right and doing God's service. He "would not have taken the course he did had he known" that Moses' instructions and reproofs came from God. "But Korah and his companions rejected light until they became so blinded" that they attributed even the most striking manifestation of God's power to human or satanic agency (*ibid.*, pp. 404, 405). The same spirit later accused Christ of casting out devils by Beelzebub (Matt. 12:24-28).

Yet Moses—whom Israel so often resisted and scorned—more than once interceded for them and turned away God's wrath, "lest he should destroy them" (Ps. 106:23).

Again, on the borders of the Promised Land when God was about to give them their inheritance, "they despised the pleasant land, they believed not his word: but murmured in their tents, and hearkened not unto the voice of the Lord" (verses 24, 25). Swayed by the negative report of the ten spies, forgetting His promises and power, they rejected the message that would have shortly put them in possession of Canaan. The price for their unbelief—forty long years of wilderness wandering and unmarked desert graves (verse 26).

One commentator has entitled this psalm "Not One

Lesson Was Learnt" (D. Kidner, *Psalms 73-150: An Introduction and Commentary*, p. 377). The next generation, instead of profiting from the mistakes of their fathers, settled down in the Promised Land, satisfied with only partial conquest. Instead of enlarging their borders and occupying new territory, they forgot God's purpose for them.

But lest we judge them too harshly—"Is not the church of today doing the same thing? With the whole world before them in need of the gospel, professed Christians congregate where they themselves can enjoy gospel privileges. They do not feel the necessity of occupying new territory, carrying the message of salvation into regions beyond. . . . Are they less guilty than was the Jewish church?"—*Christ's Object Lessons*, p. 303.

I recall listening to a group of pastors reporting their churches' territorial assignment program. A large institutional church, located in a small community with a generous Adventist population, had easily covered its territory, while some of us working the metropolitan masses struggled to reach even small segments of our population with comparatively few members. Wouldn't it be great, I mused, if busloads of our fellow believers, congregated so comfortably, could travel to our city even for a day to share in the challenge of reaching the masses.

"These things happened to them as examples and were written down as warnings for us, on whom the fulfillment of the ages has come" (1 Cor. 10:11, N.I.V.).

Ancient Israel, instead of becoming missionaries to the people around them, "mingled" among them and "learned their works. And they served their idols" (Ps. 106:35, 36). "They provoked him to anger with their inventions," even sacrificing "their sons and their daughters unto devils" (verses 29, 37).

But in spite of Israel's repeated failures, their

unfaithfulness to His covenant, "he, being full of compassion, forgave their iniquity, and destroyed them not: yea, many a time turned he his anger away, and did not stir up all his wrath. For he remembered that they were but flesh" (Ps. 78:38, 39).

Though He "abhorred his own inheritance" (Ps. 106:40), He did not deal with them as they deserved, but disciplined them at the hand of their enemies (verse 41). "Nevertheless he regarded their affliction, when he heard their cry" (verse 44). "Many times did he deliver them" when they "were brought low" by their pagan captors (verse 43). He remembered His covenant "according to the multitude of his mercies" (verse 45).

Through Israel's long history God demonstrated His covenant faithfulness over and over again. While He visited their "transgression with the rod, and their iniquity with stripes," yet He promised, "My loving-kindness will I not utterly take from him, nor suffer my faithfulness to fail" (Ps. 89:32, 33).

As we meditate on these hymns of sacred history, we may see reflected there our own failures, weaknesses, and sins—as individuals and as a church. But greater still stands "the Lord God of Israel from everlasting to everlasting" (Ps. 106:48). Because of His covenant faithfulness, we with the psalmist may appeal to Him:

"Save us, O Lord our God,
    and gather us from the nations,
    that we may give thanks to your holy name
    and glory in your praise." Verse 47, N.I.V.

Chapter 4

"The Lord Is My Shepherd"

Let me tell you about *my* Shepherd, *my* King, and *my* God.

One Sabbath morning I watched, both amused and touched, as a toddler appeared in the aisle and followed the deacons to the front of the church. Oblivious to his father's embarrassment or the congregation's gaze, the little fellow in his childish innocence knew and cared for nothing else than to be near *"my* daddy!"

Jesus Christ came to earth to demonstrate His intimacy with the Father, and to share it with us. "I and *my* Father are one" (John 10:30). "That they all may be one; as thou, Father, art in me, and I in thee, that they also may be one in us" (chap. 17:21).

But centuries before Jesus came from "the bosom of the Father" (chap. 1:18), the psalmist had declared, "He shall cry unto me, Thou art *my* father, *my* God, and the rock of *my* salvation" (Ps. 89:26).

While the psalmists delighted in declaring the greatness of their Creator, the majesty of their God, they also knew Him as a personal and faithful, covenant-keeping God. "The Lord is *my* light and *my* salvation," "*my* rock," "my help, and my deliverer" (Ps. 27:1; 28:1; 70:5).

Christians through the centuries have loved the psalms for the intensely personal approach to God that appears over and over again in them. But the psalm that

Let Me Tell You About My God

illustrates it most vividly, that grand favorite of all time, the twenty-third, tells it as no other. The "Pearl of the Psalms," as Spurgeon calls it, simple in its natural beauty and profound in its depth, speaks to the heart about *my* Shepherd.

F. B. Meyer, a nineteenth-century author, once suggested that this psalm has chased away more doubts and sorrows, comforted more poor, provided courage to more disappointed people, and poured balm and consolation into more sick hearts than there are grains of sand on the seashore. And that it will go singing on through all time till earth's pilgrims arrive safely home, and then mingle with the celestial harmonies of heaven into eternity (F. B. Meyer, *The Shepherd Psalm*, p. 15).

Throughout the Psalter we see the "Shepherd of Israel" leading His "flock," "the people of his pasture" (see Ps. 80:1; 77:20; 79:13; 95:7; 100:3). And the prophet Isaiah described the work of the Messiah in familiar words:

"He shall feed his flock like a shepherd:
  he shall gather the lambs with his arm,
    and carry them in his bosom,
      and shall gently lead those that are with young."
  Isa. 40:11.

A Persian legend tells of a certain king who reserved a small room in his palace where he kept tokens of his former life as a shepherd: the staff, the plain clothes, the water cruse. Every day he went into the room to meditate and to remember from where he had come.

Perhaps King David had a special room in his heart where he treasured the boyhood memories of his life as a shepherd. Caring for his father's flocks had taught him responsibility and prepared him for his future role as the shepherd of Israel. Surrounded only by nature on those lonely Judean hillsides, he had come to know *his*

"The Lord Is My Shepherd"

Shepherd in an intimate, enduring relationship. *to* *here*

"THE LORD IS MY SHEPHERD." David takes the perspective of the sheep itself to describe his contentment in belonging to the flock of the Good Shepherd. To appreciate fully the intimacy here, we must see the psalm in its pastoral setting. A good shepherd virtually lives with his flock, keeping constant vigil through long weary nights, on hot dry days, and in times of storm and cold. As overseer, guide, and protector—and even physician—he devotes himself to their welfare. The very survival of these helpless creatures depends on his watchful eye and strong arm. He knows each by name; he sees their individual weaknesses and vulnerabilities.

"I SHALL NOT WANT." The psalmist has the sheep imply, "My shepherd cares about me, for he owns me. He supplies all my needs. I wish you had a good shepherd like mine!"

Sheep left to graze without a human being's care soon run out of forage. A careless or hireling shepherd (one who works for pay, not for love of the flock) can bring havoc and ruin to it.

God through His prophets voiced concern about some of the false shepherds leading His people. "Woe be to the shepherds of Israel that do feed themselves! should not the shepherds feed the flocks?" (Eze. 34:2). He would require accounting of His flock at their hand. And in their place, "I will set up one shepherd over them, and he shall feed them, even my servant David" (verse 23).

And when that Shepherd came, He announced to the world, "I am the good Shepherd. . . . But he that is an hireling, and not the shepherd, whose own the sheep are not, seeth the wolf coming, and leaveth the sheep, and fleeth. . . . The hireling fleeth, because he is an hireling, and careth not for the sheep" (John 10:11-13).

Most sheep ranchers brand their sheep with a mark or initial that identifies their owner. Though painful to both the sheep and the owner, the branding process is essential for the protection of both.

"I . . . know my sheep, and am known of mine. . . . I lay down my life for the sheep" (verses 14, 15). Jesus paid the ultimate price for the privilege of purchasing and branding His flock with His own mark—the cross of Calvary.

A sense of belonging to someone who cares, someone strong enough to control our destiny, constitutes one of the deepest of human needs. "The Lord is my shepherd; I shall not want." He is my divine Manager, and I am completely satisfied with His leading and guidance.

"HE MAKETH ME TO LIE DOWN IN GREEN PASTURES." Hunger, thirst, fear, friction with other sheep, annoying parasites and pests, keep the flock in a state of irritation and restlessness. In my mind's eye I can still see my grandfather's sheep grazing and resting contentedly in a pasture not far from the garden. Yet the slightest disturbance could send them into a panic. The shepherd seeks to protect his flock from anything that would harm them, for he knows that contented sheep are healthy ones.

The dry, semiarid climates of the Middle East require painstaking effort and planning to ensure good grazing at all times. Sheep left to themselves tend to overgraze and can literally denude a pasture by eating down to the roots. Thus the careful shepherd leads his flock to new pastures at just the right time.

"HE LEADETH ME BESIDE THE STILL WATERS." Because sheep need plenty of water, they can easily get into trouble. Therefore, the shepherd has to make sure his flock does not follow its inclination to drink at parasite-filled mudholes. Instead, he finds for them clear, pure streams or wells, sometimes at great risk and inconvenience to himself.

Sometimes we human sheep act as though we lacked a Good Shepherd. We fret and worry and run in fear at every threat, or we feed in the pastures of our own choosing instead of following Him to the green ones. Stopping at infected mudholes, we expose ourselves to every kind of pollution.

The need for security—a driving motivation in the human personality—leads us to do some rather "sheepish" things. Take Kay, for example. Her endless search for security has led her to the pastures of pleasure. She goes from one barren experience to another, often stopping at the mudhole of indulgence. Her hunger and thirst never satisfied, she seems unable to recognize that the parasites of sin—broken dreams, ruined health, and an empty meaninglessness—have resulted from her failure to follow the Shepherd.

Then there's Frank. With a brilliant mind and a determined will, he insists on grazing in the dry pastures of human speculation and so-called scientific research. The mudhole of materialism fascinates him. He's so sure the water there satisfies, but already the parasites of skepticism and greed have begun eating through his soul. But, of course, sheep can't see the parasites once they get inside, so he probably won't know till it's too late.

The Good Shepherd invites all the Franks, the Kays, and you and me, "Come unto me, all ye that labour and are heavy laden, and I will give you rest" (Matt. 11:28). "I am the bread of life: he that cometh to me shall never hunger; and he that believeth on me shall never thirst" (John 6:35). "If any man thirst, let him come unto me, and drink" (chap. 7:37).

A wise shepherd will take his flock out to graze early in the morning while the dew still glistens on the grass. Sheep can actually survive without drinking water for quite some time if they get enough moisture from grazing during the night and early-morning hours.

Human sheep who spend the early-morning hours "grazing" the divine pastures also will find their spiritual thirst more than satisfied. "As the morning dew, His mercies and blessings will descend upon the suppliants."—*Testimonies*, vol. 7, p. 44.

"HE RESTORETH MY SOUL." Sometimes sheep, especially heavy ones, become "cast" or "cast down," an old English expression for a condition in which a resting sheep, because of a shift in body weight, cannot get back up on its feet. Vulnerable to predators, and with blood circulation cut off to vital organs, the helpless, frantic victim will die if not found soon by the shepherd.

David knew what it meant to be "cast" in the "horrible pit" of discouragement, defeat, and depression. His feet had slipped into the "miry clay" of doubt and despair (see Ps. 40:2). But always his shepherd would come to extricate and restore him before it was too late.

"Why art thou cast down, O my soul?
and why art thou disquieted in me?
hope thou in God: for I shall yet praise him
for the help of his countenance." Ps. 42:5.

"HE LEADETH ME IN THE PATHS OF RIGHT-EOUSNESS." Sheep are helpless animals that if left to themselves would soon perish. Unless watched over by a human being, they will ruin their pasturage and become infected with parasites from following the same trails day after day. The careful shepherd plans the best grazing for his flock, and herds them accordingly. For their own sakes, for the good of the land, and for his reputation as a good shepherd—"for his name's sake"—he leads them to better areas.

Human beings also slip into certain patterns or ruts—habits, life styles, attitudes—that stunt growth or destroy. Charles Wesley once said, "Lord, if I am tempted to nestle, put a thorn in my nest." The divine Shepherd knows we need that bit of prodding, a thorn now and then, or a gentle nudge from the shepherd's rod to keep us from nestling. No wonder the psalmist prays so often:

> "Shew me thy ways, O Lord;
> teach me thy paths." Ps. 25:4.
> "Teach me thy way, O Lord,
> and lead me in a plain path,
> because of mine enemies." Ps. 27:11.

"YEA, THOUGH I WALK THROUGH THE VALLEY . . ." Those who study the psalms have not always agreed on what the transition we apparently find here means—or if it even exists at all. Some consider it to be a shift to a different metaphor. Others see in verses 4 and 5 a description of the summer drive to the high country for better grazing, a common practice in Palestine. Working their way slowly up the mountain ranges through dark and dangerous valleys to the lusher elevations, the sheep develop a special closeness to their shepherd.

David well knew how frightening these steep rocky valleys could be to his flocks, especially when a storm raged down over them or some predator suddenly attacked them, bringing panic or even death. The shepherd's presence calms the sheep, restoring their sense of security. The closer to the shepherd, the safer they are. They know his rod as a weapon against their enemies, his staff the tangible source of their comfort. Therefore, the sheep can say with confidence:

"I will fear no evil:
for thou art with me;
thy rod and thy staff
they comfort me." Verse 4.

Many years ago, after a somewhat lengthy illness, I took a night flight from Denver, Colorado, to Lincoln, Nebraska. (The doctor had said to avoid travel by car or train.) When we neared Omaha, the crew informed us that because of heavy fog, the plane would be unable to land in Lincoln. After circling Omaha for some time, the plane finally headed toward Kansas City (several hundred miles from our destination), and landed there just before fog closed that airport. The plane's fuel supply had begun to run dangerously low.

Through the next few hours of that nightmarish experience—trying to make connections to our destinations by some other conveyance—I stayed close to another woman passenger whose garb told me she belonged to a religious order. I felt a degree of comfort and assurance in her presence that helped me get through those frightening hours.

Our Good Shepherd has promised: "Lo, I am with you alway, even unto the end of the world" (Matt. 28:20). What more could we ask?

"THOU PREPAREST A TABLE BEFORE ME." Wolves and other predators lurking in those high ranges can attack so stealthily and quickly that the sheep never see them. The shepherd, ever alert to danger, maintains a constant vigil, so that the sheep may graze "in the presence of mine enemies" (verse 5).

Fear of some lurking enemy—a verbal attack on our faith, the threat of losing a job because of our convictions, of watching evil lure our children away—all may send a chill of terror to our hearts at times, but He assures us, "Be of good cheer; I have overcome the world" (John 16:33; cf. Ps. 5:11, 12). "The way to heaven is consecrated by the Saviour's footprints. . . . His feet have pressed down the cruel thorns, to make the pathway easier for us."—*The Desire of Ages,* p. 480.

"THOU ANOINTEST MY HEAD WITH OIL." Insect pests such as flies of various kinds, gnats, and mosquitoes can wreak havoc on a flock. Swarms of tiny flies will buzz around a sheep's sensitive nose membranes, then bore into it to lay their eggs. Sheep will rub their noses into the soil, or bat their heads against trees and rocks, in desperate attempts to rid themselves of the tormenting creatures. In extreme cases a sheep can actually kill itself in its frenzied efforts for relief.

To protect his animals, the shepherd will smear or dip their heads in a mixture containing linseed oil, tar, sulphur, and other chemicals. (How well I remember the awful smell of the concoction my grandfather used on his sheep. It repels the insects and also acts as a healing agent for scab and other infections. (Sheep like to rub heads and easily pass the scab from one to another.)

Everyday annoyances and petty aggravations can in a similar way destroy our peace. They sap us of our spiritual strength. But our Shepherd brings calm to our chafed lives through the balm of the Holy Spirit, healing our fragmented existences and soothing our troubled hearts.

"MY CUP RUNNETH OVER." The more time we spend in His presence, the more we will come to know our Shepherd and the fuller will be our cup of joy and blessing. "To comprehend and enjoy God is the highest exercise of the powers of man."—*Our High Calling,* p.

61. God made us to be ever with Him.
   "Thou wilt shew me the path of life:
   in thy presence is fulness of joy;
   at thy right hand there are pleasures
   for evermore." Ps. 16:11.

   With the coming of fall, the shepherd drives his flock back to lower altitudes, where they will spend the winter. And now safely back at home, the sheep can say with confidence and assurance:

   "Surely goodness and mercy shall follow me
   all the days of my life:
   and I will dwell in the house of the Lord
   for ever." Verse 6.

*praise God our Father
Jesus our brother
Holy Spirit who takes care of us*

Chapter 5

The Lord, My Salvation

Let me tell you about the God who saves.

Like the instruments in a grand orchestra, the books of the Old Testament proclaim the message of God's love and saving power. Each player—each prophet—contributes his own unique variation of the main theme, but all blend and harmonize together to form the rich background music of the gospel.

As surely as the New Testament presents the arrival of the Messiah, so surely does the Old Testament reveal "the Lord God, merciful and gracious, longsuffering, and abundant in goodness and truth, keeping mercy . . ., forgiving iniquity and transgression of sin" (Ex. 34:6, 7). He who brought Israel out of Egypt by a "stretched out arm" (Deut. 5:15), who "redeemed" them by His "greatness" and "mighty hand" (chaps. 7:8; 9:26; 3:24), was the "mighty God, The everlasting Father, The Prince of Peace" (Isa. 9:6), born in Bethlehem's manger as "Emmanuel, . . . God with us" (Matt. 1:23).

But the Psalms, more than any other book of the Old Testament, furnish the distinct melody of the theme of salvation. The psalmist, keenly aware of his sinful nature, often cries out, "Save me, O God" (Ps. 54:1). He depends on the "Lord God of my salvation" (Ps. 88:1).

The majestic music of the Psalms is written in the key of F—faith. Faith that the sinner, though undeserving, may cast himself helplessly and hopefully on the abundant mercy of his God.

"Save thy servant that trusteth in thee. . . .
Thou, Lord, art good, and ready to forgive;
and plenteous in mercy." Ps. 86:2-5.

The tempo of the music reflects a deeply personal involvement of the psalmist with the God of his salvation:

"Help me, O Lord my salvation." Ps. 38:22.
"Thy right hand shall save me." Ps. 138:7.
"I will take the cup of salvation,
and call upon the name of the Lord." Ps. 116:13.

The refrain blends into a sweet harmony of praise for the assurance of acceptance:

"I will rejoice in thy salvation." Ps. 9:14.
"My mouth shall shew forth . . . thy salvation all the
day. Ps. 71:15.
"My lips shall greatly rejoice . . . ;
and my soul, which thou hast redeemed." Verse
23.

Several psalms—the 90th, the 103rd, the 130th, and others of the penitential prayers—help to form the major chords of this grand orchestration of the song of salvation in the Old Testament.

GOD'S ETERNITY AND MAN'S FRAILTY: PSALM 90.

"Lord, thou hast been our dwelling place in all
generations.
Before the mountains were brought forth,
or ever thou hadst formed the earth and world,
even from everlasting to everlasting, thou art God."
Verses 1, 2.

In contrast to God's greatness, the frailty and transitory nature of man, like a haunting minor refrain, surfaces often in the psalms, but nowhere more graphically than in Psalm 90. Moses' prayer contrasts the Eternal God with the vanity and futility of man's brief existence in his fallen condition.

Some time ago I stood by the graveside of a close friend of mine. A beautiful person, Winnie had given many years of her life to teaching. But the last few years for her had been a constant battle against declining health. Now the fragile thread had broken and her suffering had ended. I grieved not for her alone, but also from a deepened awareness of the shortness of life.

"Thou turnest man to destruction;

and sayest, Return, ye children of men." Verse 3.

Man's brief sojourn—seventy years, or maybe eighty "if we have the strength" (verse 10, N.I.V.)—is but as the grass that "springs up new" in the morning and "by evening it is dry and withered" (verse 6, N.I.V.). Spurgeon describes the history of grass as "sown, grown, blown, mown, gone!" *(Psalms,* on Ps. 90:6).

Even those who lived for several centuries in the early days of the human race (see Genesis 5) still returned to the dust (chap. 3:19), "for a thousand years in your sight are like a day that has just gone by, or like a watch in the night. You sweep men away in the sleep of death" (Ps. 90: 4, 5, N.I.V.). Man's life, fragile as a spider's web (the Vulgate renders verse 9, "Our years pass away like those of a spider"), perishes in the sudden, inescapable flood of death.

"We are consumed by your anger

and terrified by your indignation.

You have set our iniquities before you,

our secret sins in the light of your presence."

Verses 7, 8, N.I.V.

Man in his sinful state tends to forget either God's eternity or his own mortality. Sin itself seems to blind us to the relationship between it and death.

Let Me Tell You About My God

Mortals find it difficult to face the grim intruder, death. We never really come to grips with it till it touches our circle. Have you ever noticed how differently people express their anger in grief? Some react by denial. They refuse to accept death as a reality. They may become stoic, refusing any emotional token or release. Others reject the fact of death by imagining the dead one to be still alive in another sphere of existence. Still others vent their feelings through extreme emotional outbursts.

But faith begins with a compelling honesty about death, and more important, our sinfulness, our utter helplessness to save ourselves. It leads to a growing faith in which we constantly cast ourselves on His mercy:

"O satisfy us early with thy mercy;
that we may rejoice and be glad all our days." Verse 14.

Or as Weiser translates it, "Satisfy us . . . with thy grace."—*The Psalms: A Commentary.*

In view of this—God's wrath against sin and His mercy to the repentant:

"Teach us to number our days aright,
that we may gain a heart of wisdom." Verse 12, N.I.V.

THE GOOD NEWS: PSALM 130. Martin Luther referred to it as one of the Pauline psalms, for its few short verses contain the essence of the gospel. Beginning with an agonizing cry for mercy, the psalmist moves out of the shadows of despair into the sunlight of hope:

"Out of the depths have I cried unto thee, O Lord.
Lord, hear my voice:
let thine ears be attentive to the voice of my supplications.
If thou, Lord, shouldest mark iniquities,
O Lord, who shall stand?

But there is forgiveness with thee,
that thou mayest be feared." Verses 1-4.

When John Hinkley, Jr., attempted to assassinate President Reagan in 1981, newsmen's cameras recorded the event unerringly. His defense in court consisted not of arguing his obvious guilt, but in finding a loophole in the law.

The records of our lives stand as mute witnesses to condemn us. If the Lord should hold all our sins against us, we wouldn't stand a chance. But the psalmist pins his hopes on the good news, "There is forgiveness with thee." It is no cheap grace to squander at will, but rather that He "may be feared." "The grace of God cancels sin, but not its seriousness. Indeed, the claim of the holy God upon man's obedience, far from being reduced by His grace, only becomes weightier than ever."—A. Weiser, *op. cit.*, p. 774.

"I wait for the Lord, my soul doth wait,
and in his word do I hope. . . .
Let Israel hope in the Lord:
for with the Lord there is mercy,
and with him is plenteous redemption." Verses 5-7.

And so, like a grand suspension bridge, this psalm leads us out of the depths of despair and guilt to the final restoration of the image of God in man, when "he shall redeem Israel from all his iniquities" (verse 8).

THE HIGH COST OF SIN: PSALM 38. But underneath that bridge boils a sea of suffering, remorse, and misery, illustrated in David's tragic life. Burdened with guilt, the king schemed in vain to extricate himself from the awful net of disgrace, shame, and deception that he had woven. His intimate relationship to God alienated, his own sense of self-respect badly damaged, his influence over his family and his subjects weakened,

David lived under a cloud of depression and remorse.
> "Thine arrows stick fast in me. . . .
> There is no soundness in my flesh. . . .
> Mine iniquities are gone over mine head. . . .
> My wounds stink . . . because of my foolishness.
> I am troubled . . . ; I go mourning all day long.
> For my loins are filled with a loathsome disease. . . .
> I am feeble and sore broken." Verses 2-8.

Sin demands a terrible price. Besides the dreadful inner turmoil, David became the victim of a conspiracy and had to flee into political exile. But in spite of the darkness, his heart responded to the mercy of God:
> "I will declare mine iniquity;
> I will be sorry for my sin." Verse 18.

THE BLESSEDNESS OF FORGIVENESS: PSALM 32.
> "Blessed is he whose transgression is forgiven,
> whose sin is covered." Verse 1.

Only the bitterness of David's previous suffering matched the sweetness of his forgiveness. Now with his sin confessed, the guilt forgiven (verse 5), he rejoiced in the restored relationship:
> "Be glad in the Lord, and rejoice, ye righteous:
> and shout for joy, all ye that are upright in heart."
> Verse 11.

Only a forgiven heart can truly enter into the act of worship. Then worship becomes a time of rejoicing, of thanksgiving and praise. A time to enter into deeper fellowship and communion with God. As my pastor husband puts it, ("No worshiper should ever leave God's house with a troubled heart or without the assurance of forgiveness.")

PRAISE FOR THE LORD'S MERCIES: PSALM

103. One scholar has referred to this beautiful hymn of praise and its companion, the 104th Psalm, as "twin stars of the first magnitude" "in the galaxy of the Psalter" (D. Kidner, *Psalms 73-150: An Introduction and Commentary*, p. 364). Another writer calls it "one of the finest blossoms on the tree of Biblical faith" and one "in the great line of witnesses to God's kingdom of grace that leads from Moses and the prophets to Christ" (Weiser, *op. cit.*, p. 657).

"Bless the Lord, O my soul:
and all that is within me,
    bless his holy name.
Bless the Lord, O my soul,
and forget not all his benefits." Verses 1, 2.

David loved much because he had been forgiven much. Filled with awe at the great mercy and love of his God, his whole soul—"all that is within me"—reached out to bless God. We usually think of blessings coming *from* God to His creatures. But here the *psalmist blesses God*. What does that mean? The couplet in verse 2 explains: "Bless the Lord . . . , and forget not all His benefits." *The Jerusalem Bible* says, "Remember all his kindnesses."

Today we filled out an application for accident insurance through our employing organization. First, though, we studied carefully the benefits—due us only in case of accident or death. But every repentant sinner may realize God's benefits. The psalmist lists a few:

"WHO FORGIVETH ALL THINE INIQUITIES." Someone has well said that "we are not sinful because we sin; but we sin because we are sinful." The psalmist, conscious of his nature (see Ps. 51:5), reminds us that forgiveness includes *all* our iniquities. The hidden faults (see Ps. 19:12), the inherent weaknesses of our flesh, the warping, twisting effect of sin on our very personalities—He forgives "all thine iniquities."

The Hebrew word used here for forgiveness never appears in the context of people forgiving one another, but refers to divine pardon through atonement (see *Theological Wordbook of the Old Testament*, vol. 2, p. 626). The atonement assures us of complete removal of all our guilt.

"As far as the east is from the west,
so far hath he removed our transgressions from us."
Verse 12.

"WHO HEALETH ALL THY DISEASES." The Bible often equates sin with disease (see Isa. 1:5, 6; John 8:11). "What is pride, but lunacy; what is anger, but a fever; what is avarice, but a dropsy; what is lust, but a leprosy; what is sloth, but a dead palsy?" (quoted in Spurgeon, *op. cit.*, on Ps. 103:3).

But the healing balm of God's love casts out fear (1 John 4:18), envy, lust, hate, and every other evil infection. "For God hath not given us the spirit of fear; but of power, and of love, and of a sound mind" (2 Tim. 1:7).

"He healeth the broken in heart,
and bindeth up their wounds." Ps. 147:3.

"WHO REDEEMETH THY LIFE FROM DESTRUCTION." Sin destroys. God restores. Ultimately sin leads to the grave, but God "redeems my life from the pit [or grave]" (N.I.V.).

"The plan of redemption contemplates our complete recovery from the power of Satan."—*The Desire of Ages*, p. 311. The apostle Paul, looking forward to that final restoration, declared, "O death, where is thy sting? O grave, where is thy victory?" (1 Cor. 15:55).

"WHO CROWNETH THEE WITH LOVING-KINDNESS." The Hebrew word for *to crown* may also mean *to surround*, as in Psalm 5:12: "You surround them with your favor as with a shield" (N.I.V.).

Tall, lovely trees surround our home here in the Michigan northland. We've never taken time to identify all of them, much less count them. But protect us they do. Summer seems a little cooler. The first touches of frost usually miss our garden spot. And even the wintry blasts never hit quite as hard here. Beautiful reminders of God's mercies, they surround and protect us.

"The Lord is merciful and gracious,
    slow to anger, and plenteous in mercy." Ps. 103:8.

Again and again the psalmist rejoices in the Lord—"ready to forgive," "full of compassion," and "plenteous in mercy" (see Ps. 86:5, 15; 130:7). "From the soul that feels his need, nothing is withheld. He has unrestricted access to Him in whom all fullness dwells."—*The Desire of Ages*, p. 300.

"WHO SATISFIETH THY MOUTH WITH GOOD THINGS." "O taste and see that the Lord is good" (Ps. 34:8). The Hebrew word here means to "try the flavor of," experience for yourself. As the ads say, "Try it, you'll like it."

In their search for happiness, people sample pleasure, power, sensuality, and endless other pursuits. They may seem sweet to the taste for the moment, but they end in bitterness and emptiness. However, God offers what will permanently satisfy our deepest longings—forgiveness, acceptance, hope, and His own sweet Word (see Ps. 119:103).

"SO THAT THY YOUTH IS RENEWED LIKE THE EAGLE'S." Sin accelerates the aging process. "Grief, anxiety, discontent, remorse, guilt, distrust, all tend to break down the life forces and to invite decay and death."—*The Ministry of Healing*, p. 241. No wonder sinners preoccupy themselves in the vain search for some fountain of youth. The cosmetic industry today, one of the most lucrative in the nation, appeals to young and old, and to men as well as to women. Certain practitioners now promise instant removal of wrinkles through costly plastic surgery.

But God offers a fountain of youth at a bargain price. "They that wait upon the Lord shall renew their strength" (Isa. 40:31). "Courage, hope, faith, sympathy, love, promote health and prolong life."—*Ibid*. Positive emotions in a vital connection with God actually stimulate the nervous system and energize the whole person.

"HE HATH NOT DEALT WITH US AFTER OUR SINS." "He never treats us, never punishes us, as our guilt and our sins deserve" (verse 10, Jerusalem).

David Augsburger, in his book *The Freedom of Forgiveness*, tells the poignant story of a man whose marriage suddenly, and for no apparent reason, went sour. For ten years he patiently bore his wife's unexplained silence. Then one day, when she had had a little too much of a newly acquired "liquid friend," she began talking, and the sordid story of a longtime affair slowly unraveled. But the last straw came when he learned that a friend had been the one to betray him. All that night he struggled with rage and revenge. The next morning—not sure why—he went to church. There to greet him with outstretched hand stood his friend—the enemy. He hesitated, frozen in his bitter thoughts. Then, remembering Christ's words "Forgive us our debts, as we forgive our debtors," he slowly reached out his hand to forgive the man who had robbed him of all he held dear.

Augsburger calls him the greatest man he ever knew. Forgiveness had cost him much. To take responsibility for another's sins, to carry the load and let the guilty go free, takes divine forgiveness. Though He did no sin, "Christ . . . suffered for us" (1 Peter 2:21). He who "made him to be sin for us" (2 Cor. 5:21) "does not treat us as our sins deserve" (N.I.V.).

"LIKE AS A FATHER PITIETH HIS CHILDREN." Jesus' parable of the prodigal son illustrated the restless spirit of the sinner who sees God as stern and severe and desires to escape His restraint. Only when the prodigal returned—broken in spirit, miserable in body, and totally disillusioned with the glamor of sin—did he begin to realize how much his father had cared for him all along (see Luke 15).

The One who created us "knoweth our frame; he remembereth that we are dust" (Ps. 103:14). "The mercy of the Lord," which "is from everlasting to everlasting" supersedes both our frailty (see verses 15, 16) and our sinful nature. His salvation extends to all who "fear him" and "to such as keep his covenant . . . and remember his commandments to do them" (verses 17, 18).

Overwhelmed by God's great love and mercy, the psalmist concludes his hymn with a call for the angelic hosts and the whole universe to swell the chorus of praise (verses 20-22).

Chapter 6

The Patient Sufferer

Let me tell you about my Saviour—the patient Sufferer of the Psalms.

Why must we suffer? Human logic and wisdom fail to answer this difficult problem. Even pious religious platitudes can sound rather hollow to a body racked with unrelenting pain.

Take my friend Harold, for example, one of the most dedicated and effective ministers I've ever been associated with. But constant and severe pain, an incurable physical malady, forced him into premature retirement, a tragic loss to the ministry. How can you give a satisfying rationale for the robbed years of service and blessing? Or how brash to suggest that a godly man like Harold "needed" those years of excruciating, unbearable suffering for his character development.

The psalmists did not attempt to explain or rationalize the problem of human suffering. They merely described it—often in agonizing personal outbursts:

"In the day of my trouble I sought the Lord:
my sore ran in the night, and ceased not:
my soul refused to be comforted.
I remembered God, and was troubled:
I complained, and my spirit was overwhelmed." Ps.
77:2, 3.

God sometimes seems far away from the sufferer. The

psalmist knew all about that, too.

"Is his mercy clean gone for ever? . . .
Hath God forgotten to be gracious?
hath he in anger shut up his tender mercies?"
Verses 8, 9.

David had felt the gnawing of physical pain eating away at his life forces:

"O Lord, heal me:
for my bones are vexed." Psalm 6:2.
"My loins are filled with a loathsome disease. . . .
I am feeble and sore broken." Ps. 38:7, 8.

He knew the haunting loneliness of rejection and separation:

"Thou hast afflicted me with all thy waves.
Thou hast put away mine acquaintance far from
me." Ps. 88:7, 8.
"My lovers and my friends stand aloof from my sore;
and my kinsmen stand afar off." Ps. 38:11.

A feeling of isolation marks most suffering. Who can fully understand or share another's pain? Another's loss? Another's hurt? We may try to be sympathetic, but even our best efforts are somewhat like those of the little boy who, coming upon the scene of a serious accident, volunteers a bandaid to help the bleeding victim.

The Lord knew a bandaid wouldn't heal a bleeding, broken heart. Nor would platitudes and theories ease physical pain. So He did something drastic, something beautiful, something terribly costly. He sent His own Son to earth to become a man, to suffer and hurt with us, and finally to die as a man.

In the poignant laments of David, the singer-prophet's descriptions of his own agonies and sorrows become prophetic portraits of the Messiah. As the Son of God came clothed in the garb of humanity, so glimpses of His passion appear vested in the human experiences of

61

the suffering psalmist.

As the psalms of lament sing of sorrow, trouble, persecution, fear, guilt, and despair, so Christ came to be "in all points tempted like as we are" (Heb. 4:15), to bear in His own body our sins (1 Peter 2:24), and finally, "taste death for every man" (chap. 2:9).

> "Surely he hath borne our griefs,
> and carried our sorrows. . . .
> He was wounded for our transgressions,
> he was bruised for our iniquities:
> the chastisement of our peace was upon him;
> and with his stripes we are healed." Isa. 53:4, 5.

BETRAYAL: PSALM 41. Psalm 41 begins with a declaration that the Lord "delivers him in times of trouble," "sustain[s] him on his sickbed, and restore[s] him from his bed of illness" (verses 1, 3, N.I.V.). Things always look worse from a sickbed. Who has not felt—even in times of common or minor illness—"Will I ever feel normal again?"

The sense of sin hangs heavy on the psalmist, whether because of the state of his emotions or of the false notion that sickness somehow represents God's displeasure against the sufferer (see Job 7:18-21). At any rate, his enemies take advantage of his sickness to kick a man when he is down. "They imagine the worst" for him (verse 7, N.I.V.), and predict his death.

But still worse, "even my close friend, whom I trusted, he who shared my bread, has lifted up his heel against me" (verse 9, N.I.V.). When his son Absalom revolted against him and led a conspiracy to take his father's throne by force, one of David's close and trusted counselors, Ahithophel, joined with the conspirators (2 Samuel 15). David may have been referring to that episode, but whatever the specific incident, to have a close friend betray you and become your enemy devastates even the strongest individual.

Jesus quoted the words of Psalm 41:9 and applied them to Judas' act of betrayal: "But that the scripture might be fulfilled, He that eateth bread with me hath lifted up his heel against me" (John 13:18). For three and one-half years Judas had shared meals with Jesus, rubbed shoulders with the other eleven, and listened to Christ's teachings. He never really intended to betray Jesus; he only wished to teach Him a lesson, to test His Messiahship. But his plans backfired. The path of betrayal can lie close to the path of duty.

A trusted employee who had divulged top nuclear classified information to a foreign interest described, in a recent television interview, the gradual and subtle process by which he, once a loyal American, had turned against his country.

Our only safety—utter dependence on God through every experience of life. Even when the clouds hang low and nothing seems to make sense. Then with the psalmist we can say:

"In my integrity you uphold me
    and set me in your presence forever." Verse 12,
    N.I.V.

SAINT UNDER STRESS: PSALM 31. Psalm 31, an earnest prayer of one of God's people under stress, moves from a song of confidence and trust in "my rock and my fortress" to a plea for delivery "out of the net that they have laid . . . for me" (verse 3, 4).

"I will be glad and rejoice in thy mercy:
    for thou hast considered my trouble;
    thou hast known my soul in adversities." Verse 7.
His eyes are "consumed with grief," and his "bones grow weak" (N.I.V.). But his keen anguish, deepened by the

slander of those who seek his life, always leads him back to his "secret" place of refuge, "thy presence" (verses 9, 10, 20).

Jesus in the Garden of Gethsemane, wrestling with the terrible cup of suffering, cried out, "O my Father, if it be possible, let this cup pass from me" (Matt. 26:39). He pleaded for rescue from the fearful chasm of separation from His Father. "The fate of humanity trembled in the balance. . . . The awful moment had come. . . . Will the Son of God drink the bitter cup of humiliation and agony?"—*The Desire of Ages,* p. 690. Then with the spirit of submission that had characterized His entire life, the Saviour cried out, "Nevertheless not as I will, but as thou wilt."

Our finite minds cannot grasp the extent and depth of our Lord's suffering, yet sometimes, like the psalmist, we may catch faint hints through some personal experience.

When I think of a cup of suffering, I'm reminded of an incident that happened when I was 15 years old. My grandmother, a great believer in home cures, insisted that I consume a cup of olive oil when I suffered a sudden attack of appendicitis. The hours that followed defy description, but the next morning came part two of the "cure." A second cup of oil. That one made the first one seem like lemonade by comparison.

The cup of suffering Jesus drank in the Garden of Gethsemane was the *dread of separation* from His Father (see *The Desire of Ages,* p. 687). But the cup he took while hanging on that cruel cross *was separation* from His Father's face. "So great was this agony that His physical pain was hardly felt."—*Ibid.,* p. 753. Yet as the Saviour "drained the last dregs in the cup of human woe" (*ibid.,* p. 756), His faith penetrated the darkness of separation, and again He cried out in the words of the psalmist, "Into thine hand I commit my spirit" (Ps. 31:5).

Stephen, the first Christian martyr, breathed his last with "Lord Jesus, receive my spirit" (Acts 7:59). And through the centuries a host of other great Christians, including Luther, Melanchthon, and Huss, uttered the same words as their dying testimony. In our hour of distress and suffering we, too, may claim that same confidence and assurance, that in life or in death we may safely commit ourselves into His loving care.

"REPROACH HATH BROKEN MY HEART": PSALM 69. Listen to the agonizing cry of a tormented sufferer, alienated from friends and family because of his allegiance to God: (verses 8, 9).
> "I have come into the deep waters. . . .
> I am worn out calling for help;
> my throat is parched.
> My eyes fail,
> looking for my God.
> Those who hate me without reason
> outnumber the hairs of my head;
> many are my enemies without cause,
> those who seek to destroy me. . . .
> I am a stranger to my brothers,
> an alien to my own mother's sons." Verses 2-8, N.I.V.

Feeling his human weakness and sinfulness, he cries to God for mercy (verses 5, 13, 16). Lonely and brokenhearted, he appeals for pity, but finds none (verse 20). Then follows a vigorous venting of curses on his enemies, who deserve the worst—to be "blotted out of the book of the living"—for the suffering they have caused. Having vented his deep feelings of frustration, he pours forth a song of praise and thanksgiving to God for his deliverance (verses 29, 30).

What specific experiences in David's life prompted

such mental agony we do not know, but clearly, according to the New Testament writers, the psalmist's ordeal in a way foreshadowed the suffering Messiah.

But the cursings in verses 22-28 have troubled many. How can we reconcile such utterances to Jesus' dying prayer, "Father, forgive them; for they know not what they do"? (Luke 23:34). But notice a comparison of some of David's statements to Jesus' woes on the scribes and Pharisees in Matthew 23:

David: "Let their eyes be darkened, that they see not" (verse 23).

Jesus: "Ye blind guides" (verse 24).

David: "Pour out thine indignation upon them" (verse 24).

Jesus: "That upon you may come all the righteous blood shed upon the earth" (verse 35).

David: "Let their habitation be desolate" (verse 25).

Jesus: "Behold, your house is left unto you desolate" (verse 38).

When Jesus evicted the money-changers and merchants selling sacrifices from the Temple, His disciples remembered that it was written, "The zeal of thine house hath eaten me up" (John 2:17; Ps. 69:9). The guilty fled in terror and panic, condemned by His very presence (see *The Desire of Ages*, p. 158).

Jesus' zeal for His Father's glory made His life one of loneliness. His own nation rejected Him, His blood brothers constantly criticized Him, and His own disciples forsook Him.

On the last night before the crucifixion, as He made His way to the Garden of Gethsemane, the awful weight of the burden of sin crushed His sinless soul. The dreadful separation from God that sin brings caused Him to cry out, "My soul is exceeding sorrowful . . ." He had come into "deep waters," and in His supreme agony He longed for sympathy and comfort. But those who should have been ready to "take pity" were sleeping. He "looked for . . . comforters, but . . . found none" (verse 20). "The Saviour trod the wine press alone, and of the people there was none with Him."—*Ibid.*, p. 693. In those terrible hours "He had borne that which no human being could ever bear; for He had tasted the sufferings of death for every man."—*Ibid.*, p. 694. And when in His dying agony on the cross He made a simple request for something to assuage His thirst, those standing nearby gave Him "poison" for the "bread of consolation" (see *The SDA Bible Commentary*, on Ps. 69:21, p. 795). Where was human decency or pity that day?

THE PSALM OF THE CROSS: PSALM 22. More vividly than any other, this song of great pathos portrays the uttermost depths of suffering. Then in the closing lines it soars to the heights of praise. No recorded instance in the life of David suggests the extreme suffering described here. Whatever the actual background of its origin might have been, the prophetic depiction of the darkness of the cross and the glory of the Messiah's victory overshadows it. The Gelineau translation entitles Psalm 22 "The Suffering Servant Wins the Deliverance of the Nations." And Spurgeon suggested that "we should read reverently, putting off our shoes from off our feet, as Moses did at the burning bush, for if there be holy ground anywhere in Scripture it is in this psalm."—*Psalms*, on Psalm 22.

The psalm begins with the words uttered by Jesus in His dying agony on the cross: "My God, my God, why hast thou forsaken me?" (cf. Matt. 27:46; Mark 15:34). The anguish of a Son who knows and loves His Father intimately, yet separated from Him by a great abyss of darkness, cries out, "Why art thou so far from helping me,

Let Me Tell You About My God

and from the words of my roaring?" (verse 1; cf. Ps. 32:3).
Here is deep terror, the suffering of faith that knows God
but "cannot see the Father's reconciling face." That
anguish "pierced His heart with a sorrow that can never
be fully understood by man" (*The Desire of Ages*, p. 753).

The sufferer pauses in his tears to remember that the
holy God inhabits "the praises of Israel." He who
"dwellest between the cherubims" (Ps. 80:1), who
delivered "our fathers" will hear and have mercy (verses
3-5). It is his "island of comfort" in his "ocean of . . .
suffering" (A. Weiser, *The Psalms: A Commentary*, p.
221). But the scorn and derision continue. They "mock"
him, and "hurl insults." " 'He trusts in the Lord; let the
Lord rescue him' " (verse 8, N.I.V.). "He saved others.
. . . Let him now come down from the cross" (Matt.
27:42).

The awful beatings at His trial made "his visage . . .
marred more than any man" (Isa. 52:14). "The plowers
plowed upon my back: they made long their furrows" (Ps.
129:3).

"But I am a worm and not a man,
  scorned by men and despised by the people." Ps.
  22:6, N.I.V.

Henry Morris describes a scarlet worm (the Hebrew
word for worm may also be translated scarlet) from which
people in ancient times obtained scarlet dyes. The female
of the species would emplant her body on a tree or some
other object, her body providing sustenance and protection for her progeny until they matured. She would then
die, leaving a scarlet stain as a reminder that in dying she
had given life (*Sampling the Psalms*, pp. 113, 114).

Again the Sufferer reminds Himself that from His
mother's womb He has trusted in God, who now seems so
far away, and "there is none to help" (verses 9-11). Gaping
bulls and roaring lions surround Him (verses 12, 13).

"The mighty ones in the crowd . . . bellowed round the cross like wild cattle, fed in the fat and solitary pastures of Bashan, full of strength and fury; they stamped and foamed around the innocent One, and longed to gore Him to death with their cruelties. [See] the Lord Jesus as a helpless, unarmed, naked man, cast into the midst of a herd of infuriated wild bulls."—C. H. Spurgeon, *op. cit.*, on Ps. 22:12, 13.

Is it any wonder that his "heart is like wax", his "bones are out of joint," and he is "poured out like water" (verse 14)?

"Dogs have surrounded me;
a band of evil men has encircled me,
they have pierced my hands and my feet.
I can count all my bones;
people stare and gloat over me.
They divide my garments among them
and cast lots for my clothing." Verses 16-18, N.I.V.
(cf. Matt. 27:35).

Once more the Sufferer cries out:
"Deliver my life from the sword,
my precious life from the power of the dogs." Verse
20, N.I.V.

Suddenly the darkness lifts, the fury of the storm abates. A cry rings out, "It is finished" (John 19:30). The Sufferer of Psalm 22 bursts forth in a song of praise:

"You who fear the Lord, praise him! . . .
For he has not despised or disdained
the suffering of the afflicted one. . . .
All the ends of the earth
will remember and turn to the Lord. . . .
Posterity will serve him;
future generations will be told about the Lord.
They will proclaim his righteousness
to a people yet unborn—

for he has done it." Verses 23-31, N.I.V.

"All that He endured—. . . the agony that racked His frame, and the unutterable anguish that filled His soul at the hiding of His Father's face—speaks to each child of humanity, declaring, It is for thee that the Son of God consents to bear this burden of guilt; for thee He spoils the domain of death, and opens the gates of Paradise."— *The Desire of Ages*, p. 755.

Chapter 7

Sacrifices God Desires

Let me tell you about the sacrifices that please God.

True religion involves the whole heart and soul of man. Ancient Israel tended to substitute ritual and form. Moses, anticipating their repeated failures, posed the question "What doth the Lord require of thee, but to fear the Lord thy God, to walk in all his ways, and to love him, and to serve the Lord thy God with all thy heart and with all thy soul?" (Deut. 10;12).

Living through the cold winters of northern Michigan has taught us a new appreciation of the old-fashioned, but now popular, method of heating with wood. However, the hazards match the benefits. Always, with a wood-burning stove, there looms the real possibility of fire—uncontrolled fire in the dead of winter, far from city firefighters and equipment. And the ever-present, though less ominous, need for vigilance to keep the fire burning. Forgetfulness, failure to feed the fire sufficiently with either wood or oxygen, brings certain consequences.

So the fire of religion without form and structure, without the discipline of law, becomes a raging and uncontrolled devastation. While a religion of mere form and ritual, compliance to certain codes, without the heart and soul, is like a wood stove with the fire gone out on a blustery, frigid day in January.

The burning question "What doth the Lord require?"

Let Me Tell You About My God

appears in essence throughout the Old Testament. But nowhere does the answer ring with greater clarity than in the psalms. The outward walk—the inward love. Obedience to His commands with earnest faith in His saving acts.

CALLED TO ACCOUNT: PSALM 50. To understand God's requirements we must first recognize His sovereignty. So God reveals and identifies Himself:
"The Mighty One, God, the Lord,
    speaks and summons the earth
    from the rising of the sun to the
        place where it sets.
    From Zion, perfect in beauty,
    God shines forth." Verses 1, 2, N.I.V.
The same God who appeared at Sinai with smoke and fire (see Ex. 19:18) now appears, and "a fire devours before him, and around him a tempest rages" (verse 3, N.I.V.). He who gathered Israel at Sinai to deliver His law summons them now to judgment. Those who claim to be His covenant people He calls to account:
"'Gather to me my consecrated ones,
    who made a covenant with me by sacrifice.' . . .
"'Hear, O my people, and I will speak,
    O Israel, and I will testify against you.'" Verses
        5-7, N.I.V.
As guardians of the sacred oracles Israel had been blessed of God. The sacrificial system, as an aid to visualize the unseen and eternal, God intended should lead them "to love the Lord your God, to walk in all his ways, and to cleave unto him" (Deut. 11:22). The rite of circumcision, for example, symbolized circumcision "of your heart" (chap. 10:16).

Yet all too often, like the pagans around them, they saw the ceremonies as an end in themselves. The form

72

without the heart degenerated into an attitude of "Why need believe these crazy prophets? God cares not how we live so long as we pay our tithes. Little does He consider how we get the plunder, so long as we bring a bullock to His altar."—C. H. Spurgeon, *Psalms*, on Ps. 50:21.

No, God says, I do not rebuke you for your endless sacrifices, but for thinking that somehow you are winning My favor by performing them.

"I have no need of a bull from your stall
or of goats from your pens,
for every animal of the forest is mine,
and the cattle on a thousand hills. . . .
If I were hungry I would not tell you,
for the world is mine, and all that is in it." Verses
9-12, N.I.V.

The gods of your neighbors may depend on them for food, but do you think that "I eat the flesh of bulls, or drink the blood of goats?" (verse 13, N.I.V.).

God desires relationship above ritual. Saul, the first king of Israel, failed to learn that lesson, and it cost him his kingdom. From a strictly human viewpoint, his disobedience seems somewhat minor compared to the later moral lapse of King David. Yet God rejected Saul from being king, while He perpetuated David's throne. Does God play favorites? Or does He have a different scale for measuring sin? (see 1 Sam. 16:7).

Frustrated by waning popularity and threatened by the warring Philistines, Saul came to Gilgal for Samuel's blessing before going to battle. But when the prophet did not arrive on schedule, Saul took things into his own hands and "offered the burnt offering" (1 Sam. 13:9). As though a ceremony could of itself—like a magic wand—avert danger.

On another occasion, still bent on doing things his own way, he brought back from battle, on the pretense of offering sacrifices to God, booty that had been devoted to destruction. Samuel's answer rings down the corridors of time: "Hath the Lord as great delight in burnt offerings and sacrifices, as in obeying the voice of the Lord? Behold, to obey is better than sacrifice, and to hearken than the fat of rams" (chap. 15:22).

"Rebellion is as the sin of witchcraft" (verse 23). One of the greatest deceptions that can afflict the human mind is zeal in religious ceremony that satisfies one engaged in willful violation of God's commands (see *Patriarchs and Prophets*, pp. 634, 635). Such an attitude caused the Jewish leaders to reject Christ and to think they served God by crucifying His Son.

Pride and self-justification left no room for repentance in Saul's life. But God accepted David because of a relationship—not of ritual, but of repentance in contrast to his predecessor's defiance.

Pay your vows, says the psalmist, but remember that in the day of trouble, I am the One who delivers you, not your offerings or sacrifices (Ps. 50: 14, 15).

Then follows a stern denunciation of those who depend on religious profession to save them:

"'What right have you to recite my laws
or take my covenant on your lips?
You hate my instruction
and cast my words behind you.'" Verses 16, 17,
N.I.V.

You think that your sacrifices will cover the corruption of your hearts, the psalmist states. That your zeal for My services will hide your rebellion against My discipline. Actually, you combine "wickedness and worship" (in D. Kidner, *Psalms 1-72: An Introduction and Commentary*, p. 187) and think that because "I have kept silence" I approve. But I will not be mocked.

"Consider this, you who forget God,

or I will tear you to pieces, with none to rescue."
Verse 22, N.I.V.

Amos and Hosea, prophets to the northern kingdom of Israel, cried out against the false security of depending on sacrifices while ignoring ethical righteousness—justice, mercy, and integrity. "I will not accept them," the Lord declared (see Amos 5:22, 24; Hosea 8:13, 14). Later, both Isaiah and Jeremiah added their warnings. But their contemporary, Micah, said it best: "Wherewith shall I come before the Lord . . . ? shall I come before him with burnt offerings, with calves of a year old? Will the Lord be pleased with thousands of rams . . . ? He hath shewed thee, O man, what is good; and what doth the Lord require of thee, but to do justly, and to love mercy, and to walk humbly with thy God?" (Micah 6:6-8).

God's last message to His remnant church—Laodicea—also warns those who feel comfortable with a form of religion without the heart of it. To "lukewarm" Christians who think themselves "rich, and increased with goods, and . . . [in] need of nothing" comes the indictment of their true condition: "wretched, and miserable, and poor, and blind, and naked." "I will spue thee out of my mouth" unless you "repent" (Rev. 3:15-19).

THE SACRIFICES GOD DESIRES. "Offer the sacrifices of righteousness," the psalmist urges (Ps. 4:5). Just what sacrifices did God expect of ancient Israel? And could knowing them help Laodicea find the remedies she needs?

Under the Levitical system a sacrifice—an act of worship—expressed repentance for sin, dedication, or gratitude. The sin and trespass offerings served, in the main, for the atonement or cleansing from sin. The burnt offerings and peace offerings generally accompanied a vow (votive offering) of thanksgiving and gratitude. With

Let Me Tell You About My God

some variations and overlapping, repentance, dedication, and thanksgiving formed the basis for virtually all sacrifices. (See *SDA Bible Dictionary,* pp. 940, 941, for Table of Offerings.)

The book of Psalms interprets the Levitical system. There we may find the spiritual counterpart of the rituals and ceremonies. Some of the psalms probably were written to accompany certain sacrifices.

"A BROKEN AND CONTRITE HEART": PSALM 51. Of the seven penitential psalms, Psalm 51 is perhaps the best known and most loved, and illustrates best David's understanding of the sacrifice God desires above all.

"You do not delight in sacrifice, or I would bring it;
you do not take pleasure in burnt offerings.
The sacrifices of God are a broken spirit;
a broken and contrite heart,
O God, you will not despise." Verses 16, 17, N.I.V.

When Nathan the prophet announced to David, "Thou art the man" (2 Sam. 12:7), the king offered no self-defense, no excuses, no blaming someone else, no retaliation toward the messenger. Instead, his guilt-ridden heart broke in agonizing conviction:

"Have mercy on me, O God,
according to your unfailing love;
according to your great compassion
blot out my transgressions.
Wash away all my iniquity
and cleanse me from my sin." Verses 1, 2, N.I.V.

Such a spirit makes the sacrifice acceptable, and worship meaningful. Derek Kidner suggests that "in all this, God is looking for the heart that knows how little it deserves, and how much it owes."—*Op. cit.,* p. 194.

David certainly realized how little he deserved.

"Against you, you only, have I sinned
and done what is evil in your sight,
so that you are proved right when you speak
and justified when you judge.
Surely I have been a sinner from birth,
sinful from the time my mother conceived me."
    Verses 4, 5, N.I.V.

His heart shattered by a sense of his own sinfulness and the keen hurt he had caused the One he loved most, he cried out:

"Cleanse me with hyssop, and I will be clean;
wash me, and I will be whiter than snow. . . .
Create in me a pure heart, O God,
and renew a steadfast spirit within me." Verses 7-10
    N.I.V.

The king also knew how much he owed:

"Restore to me the joy of your salvation
and grant me a willing spirit, to sustain me.
"Then I will teach transgressors your ways,
and sinners will turn back to you." Verses 12, 13,
    N.I.V.

With his offering of a broken and contrite heart he may now approach God with the required sacrifice:

"Then shalt thou be pleased with the sacrifices of
    righteousness,
with burnt offering and whole burnt offering:
then shall they offer bullocks upon thine altar."
    Verse 19.

"I DELIGHT TO DO THY WILL": PSALM 40. As a contrite heart must accompany the sin offering, so the votive offerings required a dedicated and obedient life. But a weak and wayward people found it hard to obey. The all-wise, merciful Father, knowing the frailty of human nature, its sin-caused limitations, had prepared the ultimate, the Perfect Sacrifice:

> "Sacrifice and offering you did not desire . . . ;
> burnt offerings and sin offerings you did not
> require.
> "Then I said, 'Here I am, I have come—
> it is written about me in the scroll.
> to do your will, O my God, is my desire;
> your law is within my heart.'" Verses 6-8, N.I.V.

Paul quotes the passage to show that "this man, after he had offered one sacrifice for sins for ever, sat down on the right hand of God" (Heb. 10:12). And because of that we may have "boldness to enter into the holiest by the blood of Jesus, by a new and living way" (verses 19, 20).

Only His grace and righteousness can entitle us to the blessings of salvation (see *Selected Messages*, book 1, p. 351). But that will bring about what we of ourselves have not to give—obedience. The sacrifice of righteousness: He offers it. We accept it. And return to Him a total commitment of ourselves.

"This is the covenant that I will make with them after those days . . . , I will put my laws into their hearts, and in their minds will I write them" (Heb. 10:16). "Obedience—the service and allegiance of love—is the true sign of discipleship."—*Steps to Christ*, p. 60.

THE SACRIFICE OF THANKSGIVING. "Whoever makes thanksgiving his sacrifice honours me." Ps. 50:23, Jerusalem.

Of all the sacrifices, the gratitude offerings dominate the prayers of the psalmists, who find great delight and joy in praising God. Their thankfulness often springs from a deep sense of God's help or protection in their times of trouble or distress:

> "I will go into thy house with burnt offerings:
> I will pay thee my vows,

Which my lips have uttered, and my mouth hath
   spoken,
when I was in trouble. . . .
Come and hear, all ye that fear God,
   and I will declare what he hath done for my soul."
   Ps. 66:13-16.

Cheap praise, like cheap grace, abounds today. But genuine, deep-flowing gratitude to God under all circumstances we must learn, sometimes through our tears.

After I had spent several weeks with my parents while my father recuperated from serious surgery, the time came for the painful goodbyes under rather uncertain circumstances. Boarding an early-morning flight, I opened my small pocket Bible (N.I.V.) for comfort. Through my tears my eyes fell on the words "It is fitting for the upright to praise him" (Ps. 33:1, N.I.V.). Did God really expect praise from me in such moments of personal distress?

Ellen White states that even when reviewing the dark chapters of our experience, we should dwell on His great mercy and unfailing love, His power revealed in our deliverance. "We will praise far more than complain."—
That I May Know Him," p. 273.

"My tongue shall speak of thy righteousness
   and of thy praise all the day long." Ps. 35:28.

Ronald Barclay Allen, while writing the book *Praise! a Matter of Life and Breath,* learned that his young daughter, Rachel, had leukemia, with little hope for recovery. But from the first day of the prognosis, he and his wife determined that they would continue to praise God regardless of which way things went. They refused to wallow in their distress and grief. Later Rachel did improve, but most important, her parents praised and trusted God to do all things well.

Let Me Tell You About My God

"My voice shalt thou hear in the morning, O Lord;
in the morning will I direct my prayer unto thee,
and will look up." Ps. 5:3.

The word *direct* comes from the Hebrew word used for laying the sacrifice on the altar. "Let the fresh blessings of each new day awaken praise in our hearts for these tokens of His loving care. When you open your eyes in the morning, thank God that He has kept you through the night. Thank Him for His peace in your heart. Morning, noon, and night, let gratitude as a sweet perfume ascend to heaven."—*The Ministry of Healing*, p. 253.

In offering the sacrifice of praise—the fruit of our lips (see Hosea 14:2)—we acknowledge by our lives as well as by our words that we owe everything to our Maker. Such gratitude flows from the lips only as the result "of the Spirit's striking the cords of the soul" (*Selected Messages*, book 1, p. 344). "By him therefore let us offer the sacrifice of praise to God continually, that is, the fruit of our lips giving thanks to his name" (Heb. 13:15).

SACRIFICES FOR LAODICEA. God's call to Laodicea to "repent" invites every one of us to offer the true sacrifices of a broken spirit and a contrite heart. His counsel to purchase "gold tried in the fire" and "white raiment" suggests His willingness—really His great longing and desire—to give us the gold of faith and obedience and the righteousness of His perfect character. So that we may see to offer the sacrifice of praise and gratitude, He wants to "anoint . . . [our] eyes with eyesalve."

"The religious services, the prayers, the praise, the penitent confession of sin ascend from true believers as incense to the heavenly sanctuary, but passing through the corrupt channels of humanity, they are so defiled that

80

unless purified by blood, they can never be of value with God. . . . All incense from earthly tabernacles must be moist with the cleansing drops of the blood of Christ. He holds before the Father the censer of His own merits, in which there is no taint of earthly corruption. He gathers into this censer the prayers, the praise, and the confessions of His people, and with these He puts His own spotless righteousness. . . .

"Oh, that all may see that everything in *obedience*, in *penitence*, in *praise* and *thanksgiving* must be placed upon the glowing fire of the righteousness of Christ. The fragrance of this righteousness ascends like a cloud around the mercy seat."—*Ibid*.

Chapter 8

The Lord Knows the Way of the Godly

Let me tell you about my God—the all-wise, the all-knowing, and always fair God.

"I'm not a Christian, but I'm not a bad person, either. God would be terribly unfair to punish me, when I'm no worse than a lot of Christians I know!" A large class of people who consider themselves neither terribly bad nor unusually good follow such logic. If you were to take a poll, you'd probably find a majority placing themselves in this category. Even many Christians seem reluctant to brand themselves as "godly," but they surely don't want to be among the ungodly. So, they conclude, there must be a large third class.

TWO WAYS: PSALM 1. Yet, disturbingly, the psalms insist on only two ways. The prologue to the Psalter, Psalm 1, introduces this theme, which permeates not only the Psalms but the entire Bible.

"Blessed is the man
who does not walk in the counsel of the wicked
or stand in the way of sinners." Verse 1, N.I.V.

When the Flood came, the world contained only two groups—one inside the ark, the other outside. And when God destroyed Sodom and Gomorrah, part of a family escaped, the rest perished with the wicked inhabitants of the cities.

The Lord Knows the Way of the Godly

Jesus emphasized the same truth when he declared, "Enter ye in at the strait gate: for wide is the gate, and broad is the way, that leadeth to destruction" (Matt. 7:13).

A river has only two sides. We happen to live on the Muskegon River in our area. To get to the nearest towns or our three churches, we must cross over one of several bridges. Traveling the back roads of such wooded country along the river's winding course, one can easily become disoriented as to which side he is on. But one thing is sure: There is no third side. A person is on either the right side or the wrong.

The large majority of people who consider themselves neutral often don't know which side of the river they're traveling. They've become disoriented. But though they may not know, God does.

"For the Lord knoweth the way of the righteous: but the way of the ungodly shall perish." Verse 6.

Psalm 1 graphically presents the role model of the two ways. The godly delight in God's law (verse 2)—obedience is the hallmark of their characters. Like a "tree planted by the rivers of water," they send their roots down deep to a source of moisture that gives them life and vitality. They do not wither under the scorching sun of trials, disappointments, or sorrow. Rather, such things serve as the "divine husbandry, by which [they] grow and bring forth abundant fruit" (C. H. Spurgeon, *Psalms*, on Ps. 1:3). They prosper, not necessarily in the sense the world would consider it, but for them "all things work together for good" (Rom. 8:28).

Those who choose to live their lives apart from God appear to have unlimited freedom. But like the chaff that the wind blows about (Ps. 1:4), their lives lack purpose, meaning, and worth.

"Therefore the ungodly shall not stand." Verse 5. The

emptiness and futility of life without God can end only in final disaster and destruction (see Matt. 15:13).

The godly and the ungodly travel in opposite directions. Their goals, their life styles, their way of thinking—all spring from diametric poles. Conflict inevitably results. Jesus warned His followers to be prepared for the rift between the two ways that would cut even into families (chap. 10:34, 35). "And a man's foes shall be they of his own household" (verse 36).

Furthermore, the two ways often present complex paradoxes and illusions. The stable tree appears imprisoned by its deep roots compared to the rootless chaff, which seemingly goes where it pleases. The wicked prosper while the righteous suffer. Those who gain wealth by questionable means know all the tax loopholes, while honest, hardworking Mr. Average Citizen foots a large portion of the tax burden. Individuals who desire to control the market perpetuate the waste of precious food commodities, while hungry people go without needed nourishment. Happily married couples with good homes remain childless, while many who aren't married or can't care for their children add child to child, or worse, abort them, depriving them of life and potential adoptive couples of children. It all seems so unfair.

I shall never forget Elder Kenneth Wood, longtime editor of the *Adventist Review*, who in an around-the-fireplace conversation, observed that the most sure thing in life is that life is often unfair!

The problem of why the righteous suffer while the wicked seem to flourish, as old as the human family, caused Job to struggle through agonizing debates with his so-called friends and comforters, who tried to make sense out of a senseless situation. Misfortunes and tragedies like his often stare us in the face, defying logic and explanation.

The Lord Knows the Way of the Godly

A young man with one drink too many speeds along the highway, his perceptions fuzzy, his vision confused by his impaired judgment and the oncoming headlights. He veers into the wrong lane, instantly snuffing out one life and leaving a widow to suffer loneliness and grief as a paraplegic for the rest of her life. The drunken driver escapes with hardly a scratch.

Don and Cherryl, excited with dreams and anticipations of graduation and new jobs as church school teachers, headed home for the first Christmas of their married life. Suddenly their car careened crazily on a strip of icy pavement. A deafening crash against a bridge abutment, then deadly silence, and it was all over for two beautiful young people who had devoted their lives to God's service. All over—except for the whys.

"MY FEET HAD ALMOST SLIPPED": PSALM 73. It must have been such tormenting encounters that brought the psalmist into the depths of his despair:

"But as for me, my feet had almost slipped;
I had nearly lost my foothold." Verse 2, N.I.V.

But before describing the reason for his distress, he assures us:

"Surely God is good to Israel,
to those who are pure in heart." Verse 1, N.I.V.

Then follows a poignant account of why he almost gave up:

"For I envied the arrogant:
when I saw the prosperity of the wicked.
They have no struggles;
their bodies are healthy and strong.
They are free from the burdens common to man;
they are not plagued by human ills." Verses 3-5,
N.I.V.

In words burning with hot emotion he describes the

"carefree" wicked who seem always to "increase in wealth" (verse 12).

> "Therefore pride is their necklace;
> they clothe themselves with violence. . . .
> They scoff, and speak with malice;
> in their arrogance they threaten oppression."
> Verses 6-8, N.I.V.

Then in an outburst of anger—"God, it isn't fair!"—the psalmist expresses what most of us have felt:

> "Surely in vain have I kept my heart pure;
> in vain have I washed my hands in innocence.
> All day long I have been plagued;
> I have been punished every morning." Verses 13, 14, N.I.V.

Fred, a prosperous businessman, had tasted the good life of prestige, pleasure, and plenty. But then he came to grips with his own soul's need and gave his life to the Lord, to begin the long, lonely walk down the narrow road. Through a series of circumstances he lost his business, his wife, and his home. Reeling with shock, he, like the psalmist, asked, "What good has it done me to try to live the Christian life? I've had nothing but trouble since I accepted Christ." But like the psalmist, his own words shamed him, and he began the slow, painful process of "getting it all together."

The psalmist worries about the influence of his outbursts on the young:

> "If I had said, 'I will speak thus,'
> I would have betrayed this
> generation of your children." Verse 15, N.I.V.

Then he tells us how he put everything together again:

> "When I tried to understand all this,
> it was oppressive to me
> till I entered the sanctuary of God;

then I understood their final destiny." Verses 16, 17, N.I.V.

"The sanctuary of God"—the place and hour of worship—enabled him to sort out his fragmented thoughts and emotions. To find meaning and answers that had evaded him through mere human logic. Communion with his God brought things back into focus.

Just what the psalmist heard when he went into the sanctuary he doesn't tell us, but it could well have been David's Psalm 37, which puts the whole problem into perspective.

DON'T FRET OVER EVIL: PSALM 37.
"Do not fret because of evil men
or be envious of those who do wrong." Verse 1, N.I.V.
"Refrain from anger and turn from wrath;
do not fret—it leads only to evil." Verse 8, N.I.V.

David knew by experience that the Lord has ways of taking care of evil. Hunted by a mad king, David refused to take things into his own hands, but waited for God Himself to remove Saul and set him on the throne.

"Be still before the Lord and wait patiently for him;
do not fret when they succeed in their ways,
when they carry out their wicked schemes. . . .
A little while, and the wicked will be no more;
though you look for them, they will not be found."
Verses 7-10, N.I.V.

What matter if the "wicked plot against the righteous," drawing their swords and bending their bows (verses 12, 14, N.I.V.)—if we understand their final end, we can take it in stride:

"But the Lord laughs at the wicked,
for he knows their day is coming. . . .
Their swords will pierce their own hearts,

and their bows will be broken." Verses 13-15,
N.I.V.

Society often favors evil and caters to the wicked.
They flourish and spread themselves "like a green tree in
its native soil" (verse 35, N.I.V.), vaunting their prowess.
Ostensibly, it appears remote if not impossible that the
"power of the wicked will be broken" (verse 17, N.I.V.).

on the face of it ←

"But the wicked will perish:
The Lord's enemies will be like the beauty of fields,
they will vanish—vanish like smoke." Verse 20,
N.I.V.

When Mount St. Helens in Washington State erupted
May 18, 1980, a beautiful snowcapped mountain of
forests, lakes, and wildlife became in moments of time a
desolate waste of barren, ugly rocks and debris, as hot
molten ash gushed from the volcano. Rowe Findley, an
assistant editor for *National Geographic* and an eyewit-
ness to the tragedy, has soberly commented, "I felt a
growing apprehension for all of us living on a planetary
crust so fragilely afloat atop such terrible heats and
pressures. Never again, it came to me then and remains
with me to this day, would I regain my former
complacency about this world we live on."—*National
Geographic*, January, 1981, p. 42.

Scoffers notwithstanding, "the day of the Lord will
come," Peter declared, when the "earth . . . and the
works that are therein shall be burned up" (2 Peter 3:10).

Things are not always as they appear. That which our
dim eyes cannot now perceive and our finite minds
cannot grasp we must accept by faith. But God sees it
all—not only the end of the wicked but also the reward of
the godly:

"The days of the blameless are known to the Lord,
and their inheritance will endure forever.
In times of disaster they will not wither;

in days of famine they will enjoy plenty." Verses
    18, 19, N.I.V.

The One who formed us knows our needs and how to
fulfill them. Food, security, guidance—He provides
them all.

    "I was young and now I am old,
        yet I have never seen the righteous forsaken,
        or their children begging bread."
    "Though he stumble, he will not fall,
        for the Lord upholds him with his hand."
    "His feet do not slip."
    "They will be protected forever." Verses 25, 24, 31,
        28, N.I.V.

But best of all:
    "The righteous will inherit the land
        and dwell in it forever." Verse 29, N.I.V. (cf.
        Matt. 5:5).
    "There is a future for the man of peace." Verse 37,
        N.I.V. (cf. Matt. 5:9).

Consequently we can afford to:
    "Be still before the Lord and wait patiently for him."
        Verse 7, N.I.V.

This summer a family of great blue heron frequented
our stretch of river. We noticed that adult birds will stand
as if frozen for long periods of time till they catch their
fish. But the immature young haven't learned the art yet,
and keep on the move—inadvertently warning the fish of
their approach. To remain still before the Lord and wait
for Him when our impatience wants to make things
happen requires a maturity of spirit and a complete
surrender to Him:

    "Commit your way to the Lord;
        trust in him and he will do this:
    He will make your righteousness shine like the
        dawn,

the justice of your cause like the noonday sun."
Verses 5, 6, N.I.V.

My friend Glenda, one of the sweetest Christians I know, exemplifies such a spirit beautifully. If ever anyone had an excuse to be bitter over a marriage gone sour, she does. But instead of complaining over injustices done her, she defends the one who wronged her and teaches her children to respect their father. Instead of indulging in self-pity, she forges ahead with courage and cheerfulness to make the best of life as she finds it. She knows what it means to

"trust in the Lord and do good. . . .
Delight yourself in the Lord." Verses 3, 4, N.I.V.

To delight ourselves in the Lord may require some mental housecleaning. It may demand the removal of some of the unpleasant pictures we've allowed to hang in memory's hall—"the iniquities and corruptions and disappointments, the evidences of Satan's power" that have occupied our conversations and shadowed our thinking with the dark clouds of gloom and discouragement (*Testimonies*, vol. 5, p. 744; see also p. 610).

In their place we may "frame His mercies and blessings, and hang them in memory's hall, where we can see them and be led to offer thanksgiving to God for His goodness and love" (*The SDA Bible Commentary*, Ellen G. White Comments, on Isa. 25:1-4, p. 1143).

THE ANSWER: PSALM 73. With his mental pictures rearranged, the psalmist confesses his embarrassment at having been so foolish—"senseless and ignorant," like "a brute beast" (verses 21, 22, N.I.V.). Not that his problem has gone away! The wicked still prosper, and he continues to suffer. But with his perspective restored, his focus on eternal realities sharpened, he now endures that which before had seemed unbearable. His

The Lord Knows the Way of the Godly

faith soars above his affliction, above the transitory demands of time and earthly concerns, to the supreme and ultimate meaning in life:

"Yet I am always with you;
you hold me by my right hand.
You guide me with your counsel,
and afterward you will take me into glory.
Whom have I in heaven but you?
And being with you, I desire nothing on earth."
Verses 23-25, N.I.V.

To be with God—nothing else matters! And nothing else will seem important when we see Him face to face. All the trials, all the heartaches, and all the dark moments will vanish when we stand in His presence. But until then, His counsel will guide us, His strength will uphold us (verse 26). And like the psalmist, we may enjoy His presence here and now:

"But as for me, it is good to be near God.
I have made the Sovereign Lord my refuge;
I will tell of all your deeds." Verse 28, N.I.V.

Chapter 9

I Delight in His Law

Let me tell you about the law of my God, my delight and my meditation.

"O how love I thy law!" Ps. 119:97.

WHO CAN ENTER GOD'S TEMPLE?: PSALM 15. Picture a band of Israelite pilgrims approaching the Temple gate. They have come for one of the great festivals to worship God at His "holy hill" of Zion. Standing at the gate, they ask for admittance with the question "Who may enter His glorious presence?"

"Lord, who may dwell in your sanctuary?
Who may live on your holy hill?" Ps. 15:1,
    N.I.V.

"Who may ascend the hill of the Lord?
Who may stand in his holy place?" Ps. 24:3,
    N.I.V.

The officiating priests, who represent God to the people, answer them. But their responses differ strikingly from what some of Israel's heathen neighbors might expect to hear at their temples. They make no mention of sacrifices, no ritual exercises, not even the bringing of offerings. Instead, the pilgrims hear described the type of citizen God will accept in His sanctuary:

"He whose walk is blameless

and who does what is righteous,
who speaks the truth from his heart." Ps. 15:2,
N.I.V.
"He who has clean hands and a pure heart,
who does not lift up his soul to an idol
or swear by what is false." Ps. 24:4, N.I.V.

Anyone worships God in vain who "slanders" his neighbor or "slurs" his fellow men (Ps. 15:3, N.I.V.), or who brings an offering in one hand while with the other he accepts "a bribe against the innocent," or grows rich from usury (verse 5, N.I.V.). No, the man whom God accepts must have "clean hands" and a pure heart that refuses to compromise with evil under any circumstances. He must be a man of integrity, keeping his promises "even when it hurts" (verse 4, N.I.V.).

"Blessed are the pure in heart: for they shall see God" (Matt. 5:8). Jesus taught and demonstrated that such conduct applies even to our enemies (verses 42-45). "Therefore all things whatsoever ye would that men should do to you, do ye even so to them: for this is the law and the prophets" (chap. 7:12).

Does God offer salvation through forgiveness and justification on the one hand, while giving us an impossible code of conduct and ethics on the other?

No, the One who cleanses from sin also enables His children to walk in His ways—the path of obedience to His holy law and will. Though we can never earn a right to heaven by doing anything, He promises guidance and direction as one of the benefits of salvation. And that includes control of the hands, the feet, the tongue, the eyes, and most important—the will.

Yet as a God of truth and equity He respects our right of choice. So all who desire to walk in His way must constantly choose His control. The psalmist David understood the importance of making such decisions and expressing them openly.

A KINGLY RESOLVE: PSALM 101. David wrote, probably early in his reign, of his determination to conduct his affairs, both private and public, according to the principles of integrity, justice, and purity. He began where all of us should begin—his own home:
"I will walk in my house with blameless heart."
Verse 2, N.I.V.
"If religion is to influence society, it must first influence the home circle. . . . If there were more genuine home religion, there would be more power in the church. . . . Angels delight in a home where God reigns supreme."—*The Adventist Home*, pp. 318-322.

Had David lived up to his own ideal, how different his life, especially the later years, might have been! He would have averted much sorrow and tragedy.
"I will behave myself wisely in a perfect way. . . .
I will set no wicked thing before mine eyes."
Verses 2, 3.

Ellen White once commented that when the daily paper came into her home, she felt as though she wanted to hide it. "It seems as if the enemy is at the foundation of the publishing of many things that appear in newspapers. Every sinful thing that can be found is uncovered and laid bare before the world."—*Ibid.*, p. 404. What might she say should she witness the actual televising of "every sinful thing" into our living rooms? If we would have that wisdom which is from God, we must become fools in the sinful knowledge of this age, shutting our eyes and our ears to the blatant evil around us.

We had never owned a television set until we became involved with the It Is Written telecast. When we brought home a small set purchased at a garage sale, we sensed its evil potential. So we typed the words of this

psalm on a three-by-five-inch card and placed it in the
corner of the screen as a reminder to ourselves and others
who came under our roof:

"I will set before my eyes
　　no vile thing. . . .
No one who practices deceit
　　will dwell in my house;
no one who speaks falsely
　　will stand in my presence.
Every morning I will put to silence
　　all the wicked of the land;
I will cut off every evildoer
　　from the city of the Lord."
　　　　　　　Verses 3-8, N.I.V.

THE LAW OF THE LORD: PSALM 119. Though
David sometimes failed to live up to his high resolves, he
nevertheless loved God's law, convinced that the path of
obedience alone brings true happiness. Significantly, his
meditations on the subject comprise the longest chapter
in the Bible. A giant among the psalms, appearing in the
very center of Scripture, it has sometimes been called a
little Bible.

"Blessed are they whose ways are blameless,
　　who walk according to the law of the Lord."
　　　　Verse 1, N.I.V.
"Your word is a lamp to my feet
　　and a light for my path." Verse 105, N.I.V.

Spurgeon tells of a man whose life was saved by the
length of Psalm 119. About to die at the scaffold, he chose
it to be sung before his excution (according to the custom
of that day). About two thirds of the way through it a
pardon arrived—just in time.

An acrostic poem, Psalm 119 contains twenty-two
strophes, or stanzas, one for each of the twenty-two

letters of the Hebrew alphabet. Each of the eight lines in a strophe begins with the same letter. Thus the lines of verses 1-8 begin with the Hebrew *aleph*, verses 9-16 with *beth*, et cetera. (Consequently, the thought sequence does not follow a logical pattern.)

The psalmist uses eight words interchangeably to describe the pathway of obedience: law, commandment, precept, statutes, judgment, testimony, and word. While they have different shades of meaning, they all describe God's revealed will and instruction—His whole body of teaching—contained in His Written Word, including His moral law, the Ten Commandments. Each strophe contains a variety—if not all of the words—often used interchangeably.

Rather than being a legalistic extolling of the law (as some see it), it reveals the heart of one who loves the Lord and His law, and who realizes his total dependence on a power outside himself to follow it.

Perhaps a thought profile of Psalm 119 will best serve to give us an insight into the psalmist's deeply spiritual feelings, as well as to focus on the lessons it holds for Christians desiring to walk the path of obedience.

"THY TESTIMONIES ALSO ARE MY DELIGHT" (VERSE 24). The psalmist declares his great pleasure in God's law no less than nine times (cf. Ps. 40:8). Seven times he expresses his love for it, and three times its preciousness. God's words are "sweeter than honey" to his mouth (verse 103), and he values the commandments more than "fine gold" (verse 127; cf. Ps. 19:10). He hides the word in his heart (verse 11). Food left on the shelf eventually spoils if bugs or mice don't find it first, but that taken into the body nourishes and satisfies.

The word *delight* in the Bible frequently expresses deep emotional feeling and satisfaction. What pleases the tongue more than the sweetness of honey? What encourages the soul more than the precious promises of His Word? The more we meditate on God's Word, the more things we will see in it to delight our souls.

The psalmist utters praise or thanksgiving for God's precepts eight times, while six verses mention them as his favorite meditation.

"Seven times a day do I praise thee." Verse 164. He anticipates the night watch as an opportunity for communion with God:

"At midnight I will rise to give thanks unto thee." Verse 62.

The next time you have trouble sleeping, try memorizing Psalm 119, or read it and meditate on each verse.

"QUICKEN ME IN THY RIGHTEOUSNESS" (VERSE 40). The psalmist repeatedly prays to be "quickened" (or acknowledges that God has done it) by His lovingkindness (verses 88, 159), his righteousness (verse 40), or by His word (verses 25, 50, 107). The word *quicken* translates from a Hebrew word meaning to live or to make alive. Only the New Testament would fully develop the hint of the psalmist here—when Jesus declared that a man must be born again (John 3), and when Paul taught that the old nature must die (Rom. 6:6), giving way to a new creature in Christ Jesus (2 Cor. 5:17).

Many years ago a Wesleyan missionary, while translating the Bible into the local language of a tribe in Northern Rhodesia, decided one morning to read to his congregation a chapter from his new translation. Overjoyed at hearing the message in their own language for the first time, the people insisted that he continue reading. "Let God go on talking to us. He speaks our language!"—Walter B. Knight, *Three Thousand Illustrations for Christian Service*, p. 57. Yes, the Word quickens because it speaks God's message in our language, gripping us at the very core of our being.

Six times the psalmist pleads for God's salvation:

"Save me, and I shall keep thy testimonies." Verse 146.

"I SHALL KEEP THY LAW" (VERSE 34). Thirteen times the psalmist resolves to keep the commandments, but his determination results from the quickening (verse 88) or as his heart is enlarged (verse 32) or in answer to his prayer "Save me" (verse 146). He realizes how easily his human nature forgets. Ten times he promises:

"I will not forget thy word." Verse 16.

Sensing a need to be taught of God, nine times he prays,

"Teach me, O Lord, the way of thy statutes." Verse 33.

His success he attributes to God:

"I have not departed from thy judgments: for thou hast taught me." Verse 102.

Too many Christians live by the humanistic rule of doing "what is right for me." How fortunate is the Christian who knows in his heart that he follows God's will according to the written directions.

Nine times in Psalm 119 David recognizes that affliction has been a hard but good teacher:

"Before I was afflicted I went astray." Verse 67.

"It is good for me that I have been afflicted; that I might learn thy statutes." Verse 71.

The rush of living, business interests, and carelessness in devotional matters had slowly but surely eroded Joe's spiritual life until he found himself far from God and his church. Then one day tragedy struck. His only son—the apple of his eye—was suddenly and needlessly snatched from him. The loss shook him to the core—it drove him to his knees and back to the God his son had dedicated his life to serve. Today Joe is a pillar in his church and a witness to the community of the blessings that can come even out of affliction.

Eight times the psalmist prays for understanding:
"Make me to understand the way of thy precepts." Verse 27.

God has granted his request, and made him "wiser than . . . [his] enemies" and given him "more understanding" than his "teachers" or the "ancients" (verses 98-100).

"THEY HAVE MADE VOID THY LAW" (VERSE 126). In ten references the psalmist's distress over the wicked who transgress God's law causes him grief (verse 158) and brings rivers of tears (verse 136).

Legend has it that a certain princess, who had never seen herself, sent for a missionary who had a magic looking glass. She wanted to see the dazzling beauty that others had told her she possessed. But the coveted mirror revealed only a hideously ugly creature. Shocked and angered, the princess smashed the mirror to bits with her royal fist and had the missionary banished (*ibid.*, p. 67). Many moderns hate God's mirror because it shows them themselves. But rather than repent, they try to remove God's holy law out of existence.

Evil may affect the child of God in one of two ways. Either it makes him less sensitive to sin, leading to a spirit of compromise with evil, or it drives him to appreciate God's law even more as he sees the contrast between His righteous character and the despicable nature of sin.

"Those who make the Word of God the man of their counsel will esteem the law of God, and their appreciation of it will rise in proportion as it is set aside and despised. Loyal subjects of Christ's kingdom will reecho the words of David and say, 'It is time for thee, Lord, to work: for they have made void thy law [verse 126]."—*The SDA Bible Commentary*, Ellen G. White Comments, on Ps. 119:126, 127, p. 1152.

"GREAT ARE THY TENDER MERCIES, O LORD" (VERSE 156). In at least twenty verses the psalmist extols God's character with words like *mercy, kindness, lovingkindness, good, faithful, righteous,* and *love*. Because the Word and His revealed will express His very nature, the psalmist in another twenty verses describes the law as *righteous, faithful, eternal, broad, enlightening, pure, true,* and *precious*—the same attributes that depict God Himself.

"The more we search the Bible, the deeper is our conviction that it is the word of the living God, and human reason bows before the majesty of divine revelation."—*Education*, p. 170.

"GREAT PEACE HAVE THEY WHICH LOVE THY LAW" (VERSE 165). Such an understanding of the character of God and its relation to His Word, the concept of obedience based on a response of love made possible by the quickening power of God's Spirit in the life, enables a man to "walk at liberty" (verse 45), free from the chains of guilt, remorse, malice, hatred, revenge, and prejudice.

For years Mary had struggled with the sins of fault-finding and criticism, never quite gaining the victory. Then one day she discovered a sack of old hostilities and resentments—like a bag of unemptied garbage shoved in a far corner of a closet—hidden in the deep recesses of her soul. Musty with age and unsightly to behold, they had to be disposed of immediately. She would accomplish nothing by examining them or identifying their source. Recognizing that fact and surrendering them to the One who alone could remove them brought her victory at last. And with the victory came peace of mind.

> "Great peace have they which love thy law:
> and nothing shall offend them." Verse 165.

To love God's law results in the deep heart-searching activity of the Holy Spirit in our inner lives. Though it is painful to have the deformities of the soul laid bare, the rewards free the soul and bring peace. "Sin can triumph only by enfeebling the mind, and destroying the true liberty of the soul. Subjection to God is restoration to one's self—to the true glory and dignity of man."—*The Desire of Ages*, p. 466.

Our homes and our families, the church, and the wider circle in which we move will all feel the influence of God's law in our lives. "If the law of God is obeyed, the demon of strife will be kept out of the family, and no separation of interests will take place, no alienation of affection will be permitted."—*The Adventist Home*, p. 106.

"INCLINE MY HEART UNTO THY TESTI-MONIES" (VERSE 36). Perhaps the most poignant of all this great psalm's prayers are the psalmist's yearnings for guidance. *To incline* means "to turn toward." He realizes that unless God turns his heart to do right, his natural bent will lead him down the path of least resistance. Fourteen times he utters such prayers as:

> "O that my ways were directed to keep thy statutes!"
> Verse 5.

> "My soul breaketh for the longing
> that it hath unto thy judgments." Verse 20.

And the psalm ends with an acknowledgment of his utter dependence on God:

> "I have gone astray like a lost sheep;
> seek thy servant; for I do not forget thy

commandments." Verse 176.

Sinful man cannot observe a perfect law. But a perfect Redeemer did. "It was His mission, by making men partakers of the divine nature, to bring them into harmony with the principles of the law of heaven."— *Thoughts From the Mount of Blessing,* p. 50.

The psalmist understood the New Testament promise, "I will put my laws into their mind, and write them in their hearts" (Heb. 8:10). Having experienced it, the psalmist could say with confidence some thirteen times:

"My soul hath kept thy testimonies." Verse 167.

"I have chosen the way of truth." Verse 30.

"I . . . delayed not to keep thy commandments." Verse 60.

He is not ashamed of his way of life, but "will speak . . . before kings" (verse 46).

"Thy statutes have been my songs
in the house of my pilgrimage." Verse 54.

"Accept . . . the freewill offerings of my mouth, O Lord." Verse 108.

"My tongue shall speak of thy word:
for all thy commandments are righteousness." Verse 172.

Chapter 10

God, the Righteous Judge

Let me tell you about my God, the righteous Judge.
"The Lord is known by his justice." Ps. 9:16, N.I.V.
"Help, my lord, O king" (2 Kings 6:26). The bitter cry
from a woman in great distress reached the ears of the
king of Israel as he walked along the wall surrounding his
besieged city, famine-stricken and desperate. Two
starving women had agreed to eat their sons. Now with
the first victim gone, the other woman had hid her son.
The anguished mother begged for justice for the
gruesome crime and deception. But the helpless king,
turning and tearing his garments, could offer nothing
more than: "If the Lord does not help you, where can I get
help for you?" (verse 27, N.I.V.).

Fifteen-year-old Nguyen Phuong Thuy escaped with
sixty-seven other refugees from Vietnam, only to have the
crew of a Thai fishing boat kidnap her. After watching her
sister and the others drown, she and one other young girl
endured months of terrible, subhuman atrocities by
pirates on fifteen different fishing boats. Finally, after
being set ashore, Thai authorities jailed her as an illegal
immigrant (*These Times*, September, 1982, p. 8).

A widow, robbed of all her husband left her—perhaps
by a smooth-tongued manipulator—stood before the

judge crying, "Help me against mine adversary" (Luke 18:3, marginal reading). But her plea for justice fell on uncaring ears.

An elderly couple had invested their entire hard-earned life's savings with a fast-talking entrepreneur. Then one day he suddenly dropped out of the picture, leaving wife, family, business partners, and many hapless investors holding the bag. The vain requests for justice received only responses of "Too bad!"

"HELP, LORD—HOW LONG?": PSALMS 10-14.
"Help, Lord; for the godly man ceaseth;
for the faithful fail from among the children
of men.
They speak vanity every one with his
neighbour:
with flattering lips and with a double heart do
they speak." Ps. 12:1, 2.

The Hebrew word used here for "help" has the meaning of "rescue" and save, sometimes used in connection with military assistance. It often appears in the setting of a cry for justice, as in this passage.

Help! The cry against cruelty, oppression, deception, and injustice all too often meets with indifferent or impotence. Even God seems far away at times:

"Why, O Lord, do you stand far off?
Why do you hide yourself in times of trouble?"
Ps. 10:1, N.I.V.

The wicked man "persecute[s] the poor" (verse 2) and, boasting of his lust, blesses the greedy. Haughty and self-confident, he lies, curses, threatens, deceives, and snares his victims, and practices violence. He ignores God's laws, sure that He neither sees nor cares (see verses 2-11, N.I.V.).

Justice often seems slow in coming:
> "How long wilt thou forget me, O Lord? for ever?
> how long wilt thou hide thy face from me?" Ps. 13:1.

Yet the psalmist can say:
> "But I have trusted in thy mercy;
> my heart shall rejoice in thy salvation." Verse 5.

Faith penetrates beyond his despair and rests in the confidence that a righteous Judge will eventually vindicate the cause of the oppressed.
> "The Lord shall cut off all flattering lips,
> and the tongue that speaketh proud things. . . .
> For the oppression of the poor,
> for the sighing of the needy,
> now will I arise, saith the Lord." Ps. 12:3-5.

The psalmist's ultimate faith that right will prevail does not lessen the intensity of the struggle he feels as he encounters the hostility of the wicked.
> "If the foundations be destroyed,
> what can the righteous do?" Ps. 11:3.

The conflict between good and evil, with its roots in the Garden of Eden (Gen. 3:15), has ravaged God's children through the ages. It caused Cain to kill Abel, led Joseph's brothers to sell their own flesh and blood into slavery, and prompted an insane crowd to choose a murderer in place of an innocent Man whom they condemned with "Crucify him, crucify him!" (see Matt. 27:22, 23).

The same Christ who taught us to love our enemies also reminded us that He came not to send peace but a sword. His enemies dogged His every step. The archrebel who asserted, "I will exalt my throne above the stars of God" (Isa. 14:13), rallied all the weapons of hell against the Son of God as He walked among men (see *The Desire of Ages*, p. 116). Yet He could say while bearing the brunt of the conflict, "The prince of this world cometh, and hath nothing in me" (John 14:30).

The wicked thinks God has forgotten (see Ps. 10:4, 11), and ultimately denies Him altogether:

"Our lips are our own:
who is lord over us?" Ps. 12:4.
"The fool hath said in his heart,
There is no God." Ps. 14:1.

What may seem like a kind of preoccupation with his wicked enemies (as some see the psalms of judgment) indeed become prophetic glimpses of the great struggle between good and evil, with emphasis on the final judgment passed on evildoers by a righteous God:

"The Lord trieth the righteous:
but the wicked and him that loveth violence
his soul hateth.
Upon the wicked he shall rain snares,
fire and brimstone, and an horrible tempest:
this shall be the portion of their cup." Ps. 11:5, 6.

"THAT MEN MAY KNOW": PSALMS 58, 79, 83. The psalms of imprecation—curses on wicked enemies—disturb and dismay many people, even some students of the Psalter. It's one thing for God to pass judgment on the wicked, but does the psalmist have that right? Or do his outbursts represent battle-line skirmishes faced by every child of God against the evil within and without? (see Eph. 6:11-13).

"The wicked are estranged from the womb. . . .
Their poison is like the poison of a serpent. . . .
Break their teeth, O God, in their mouth." Ps. 58:3-6.

Justice demands that wrongs be righted, that violence be weighed (verses 1, 2), that the lawless who refuse to pay heed (verse 5) and continue to break the law be stopped and punished.

Suppose you had lost two of your children to careless

drunken drivers who got off with only a few months in jail and probation? Would you then appreciate better the wish for God to break the teeth of evil? And maybe even help Him by joining an organization like MADD—Mothers Against Drunken Drivers?

"The righteous shall rejoice when he seeth the
   vengeance:
he shall wash his feet in the blood of the wicked."
   Verse 10.

The revelator echoes the thought when he has the souls under the altar cry out, "How long, O Lord, . . . dost thou not avenge our blood on them that dwell on the earth?" (Rev. 6:10).

No, the psalmist's imprecations against the wicked harbor no mere personal vendetta. Rather, because he loves the right and the good, he longs to see God's judgment break the cruel power of the enemy.

" 'So' people will say 'the virtuous do have their
   harvest;
so there is a God who disperses justice on earth!' "
   Ps. 58:11, Jerusalem.

Psalm 79 describes in pathetic terms an attack by the heathen on God's inheritance:

"Thy holy temple have they defiled;
   they have laid Jerusalem on heaps. . . .
We are become a reproach to our neighbours,
   a scorn and derision to them that are round about
   us." Verses 1-4.

A disgruntled church member brings a lawsuit against the church, and it hits the headlines of nearly every major newspaper. Someone writes a book attacking a basic pillar of faith, and the network wires buzz with glee. To the psalmist, an attack on God's people means defiance against God Himself. He appeals to the Lord not to keep silence (Ps. 83:1).

> "For, lo, thine enemies make a tumult:
> and they that hate thee have lifted up the head.
> They have taken crafty counsel against thy people,
> and have consulted against thy hidden ones.
> They have said, Come, and let us cut them off
> from being a nation;
> that the name of Israel may be no more in
> remembrance." Verses 2-4.

Delighted with Israel's disgrace, the pagans taunt, "Where is their God?" (Ps. 79:10). And the distressed child of God pleads, "Let them know who You are!"

> "Help us, O God of our salvation,
> for the glory of thy name:
> and deliver us, and purge away our sins,
> for thy name's sake." Verse 9.

The psalmist's stern denunciations, his wish that God's judgments be meted out on those who hate Him, harbors no personal revenge. He hopes that somehow they may be led to "seek thy name, O Lord" (Ps. 83:16). But if not, by their demise,

> "that men may know that thou, whose name alone is
> Jehovah,
> art the most high over all the earth." Verse 18.

In the light of the judgment, righteousness must be exalted and sin ultimately destroyed. The wicked must repent or perish. God's name and honor must be vindicated before the universe.

"HE SHALL JUDGE THE WORLD IN RIGHTEOUSNESS": PSALMS 9, 94. But all too often it seems that "judgment is turned away backward, and justice standeth afar off: for truth is fallen in the street, and equity cannot enter" (Isa. 59:14). And the oppressed cry out:

"How long shall the wicked triumph?" Ps. 94:3.

God, the Righteous Judge

But the psalmist assures,
"He shall judge the world in righteousness,
he shall minister judgment to the people in
uprightness." Ps. 9:8.
"He hath prepared his throne for judgment." Verse
7.

To many the idea of judgment brings fear and trembling, as it did to Felix in Paul's day (see Acts 24:25), but the psalms associate it with rejoicing and gladness (see Psalm 98). The Hebrew word for *judge* or *judgment* has the basic meaning of exercising the processes of government. The term *throne* similarly implies authority, royal power, or government. The psalms depict God's government as based on equity, truth, and righteousness, with God as the supreme and rightful ruler.

"Thy righteousness is like the great mountains;
thy judgments are a great deep." Ps. 36:6.

Spurgeon comments on this verse: "Who can bribe the Judge of all the earth, or who can, by threatening, compel Him to pervert judgment? Not even to save His elect would the Lord suffer His righteousness to be set aside. . . . Right across the path of every unholy man who dreams of heaven stands the towering Andes of divine righteousness, which no unregenerate sinner can ever climb."—*Psalms*, on Ps. 36:6.

God is always willing to forgive the sinner, but He cannot and will not tolerate evil, because sin destroys. It has only one ultimate outcome.

"The heathen are sunk down in the pit that
they made. . . .
The wicked is snared in the work of his own
hands." Ps. 9:15, 16.

He who lives by hate and violence will likely die by the same. During the horrors of the French Revolution, everyone implicated in the gruesome death of Queen

109

Let Me Tell You About My God

Marie Antoinette—judges, jury, prosecutors, and witnesses—perished by the guillotine within nine months of her execution.

God's vengeance is not only just but merciful. To allow sin to continue would erode the happiness of the universe and finally extinguish it. The judgment of the wicked brings "destructions" "to a perpetual end" (verse 6). The pollution, the ravages, the perversions that sin has inflicted, even on nature, God must totally and completely eradicate from His universe, or it can never be the joyous place He created it to be.

While retribution of evil looms large and certain in the Psalms, another aspect of judgment emerges with equal force—the defense of the righteous:

> "Who will rise up for me against the evildoers?
> or who will stand up for me against the workers of
> iniquity?
> Unless the Lord had been my help,
> my soul had almost dwelt in silence." Ps. 94:16,
> 17.

"The Lord is known by the judgment which he executeth" not only on the wicked; "the needy shall not always be forgotten: the expectation of the poor shall not perish for ever" (Ps. 9:16, 18). He judges "the fatherless and the oppressed" (Ps. 10:18), the widows (Ps. 68:5), and the poor (Ps. 72:2; 109:31).

According to Solmon's dedicatory prayer, an accused suppliant might seek refuge in the temple, and expect God to "declare the innocent not guilty, and so establish his innocence" (1 Kings 8:32, N.I.V.).

After David had patiently suffered the curse of Cush the Benjamite, rather than avenging himself as he might have done, he prayed for God to judge his innocence:

> "My defence is of God,
> which saveth the upright in heart.

God judgeth the righteous,
and God is angry with the wicked every day."
     Ps. 7:10, 11.

David could afford to "let the enemy persecute . . . [his] soul" and "lay . . . [his] honour in the dust," for he knew that one day the records would be set straight, and the "mischief shall return upon his own head" (verses 5, 16). Therefore, he could "praise the Lord according to his righteousness" (verse 17).

In the ancient sanctuary service the high priest wore the "breastplate of judgment" over his heart "continually" (Ex. 28:29, 30), illustrating beautifully the intercessory phase of the judgment. Containing the names of the twelve tribes, the breastplate signified the closeness of the intercessor to his people.

He who has "entered . . . into heaven itself, now to appear in the presence of God for us," "ever liveth to make intercession" for us (Heb. 9:24; 7:25). "We have an advocate with the Father, Jesus Christ the righteous" (1 John 2:1).

The psalmist cherished the sweet reassurances he found at the altar of God in the sanctuary:

"And they that know thy name will put their trust
     in thee:
  for thou, Lord, hast not forsaken them that seek
     thee."
     Ps. 9:10.

"Then will I go unto the altar of God,
  unto God my exceeding joy:
  yea, upon the harp will I praise thee, O God my
     God."
     Ps. 43:4.

FEAR GOD . . . GIVE GLORY . . . WORSHIP HIM: PSALM 96. Picture, if you will, the judgment scene in the heavenly sanctuary:

> "Thrones were set in place,
> and the Ancient of Days took his seat.
> His clothing was as white as snow;
> the hair of his head was white like wool.
> His throne was flaming with fire,
> and its wheels were all ablaze.
> A river of fire was flowing,
> coming out from before him.
> Thousands upon thousands attended him;
> ten thousand times ten thousand stood before him.
> The court was seated,
> and the books were opened." Dan. 7:9, 10, N.I.V.

The "accuser of our brethren" (Rev. 12:10) claims all of earth's inhabitants as his subjects and deserving of God's wrath. But for those who have chosen to trust in the heavenly Advocate, judgment becomes release and deliverance. Their Judge also acts as their Defense. The prophet Daniel watched as a persecuting power waged "war against the saints and defeating them, until the Ancient of Days came and *pronounced judgment in favor of the saints* of the Most High, and the time came when they possessed the kingdom" (Dan. 7:21, 22).

But before they can possess the kingdom, the good news—the everlasting gospel, that the Judge defends those who place their cases in His hands—must go to "every nation . . . kindred . . . tongue, and people, saying with a loud voice, Fear God, and give glory to him; for the hour of his judgment is come: and worship him that made heaven, and earth, and the sea, and the fountains of waters" (Rev. 14:6, 7).

As John the revelator beheld the awful judgments of wrath about to fall on the unrepentant, he heard in vision the final glorious new song of the victors: "Great and marvellous are thy works, Lord God Almighty; just and true are thy ways, thou King of saints. Who shall not *fear*, thee, O Lord, and *glorify* thy name? for thou only art holy: for *all nations* shall come and *worship* before thee; for thy *judgments* are made *manifest*" (chap. 15:3, 4).

The psalmist may not have seen it as graphically as did the revelator, but sing of it he did:

"O sing unto the Lord a *new song*. . . .
Declare his *glory* among the heathen,
his wonders among all people.
For the Lord is great,
and greatly to be praised:
he is to be *feared* above all gods.
For all the gods of the nations are idols:
but the *Lord made the heavens*. . . .
Give unto the Lord the *glory due* unto his *name*. . . .
O *worship* the Lord in the beauty of holiness:
fear before him, all the earth. . . .
For he cometh to judge the earth:
he shall *judge* the *world* with *righteousness*,
and the people with his truth." Ps. 96:1-13.

Chapter 11

God, My Refuge in the Time of Trouble

Let me tell you about my God—my Help and my Refuge in the time of trouble.

God's people stand on the very "threshold of the crisis of the ages" *(Prophets and Kings,* p. 278). More surely than any other generation we face the inevitable truth, that "all that will live godly in Christ Jesus shall suffer persecution" (2 Tim. 3:12). As the spiritual warfare of the ages hurtles to a dramatic finale, "the devil is come down unto you, having great wrath, because he knoweth that he hath but a short time" (Rev. 12:12). He attacks from both within and without the church. With his roar (1 Peter 5:8) he seeks to paralyze the inhabitants of the earth with fear so that they become easy prey to his deceptions.

The "great changes . . . soon to take place in our world" (written at the turn of the century; *Testimonies,* vol. 9, p. 11) have already occurred. The byproducts of man's technical advances, like a Damoclean sword, hang over our heads by a thread, which the anger and unrestrained passions of men or nations could break at any moment.

The strained intensity "taking possession of every earthly element" declares "that something great and decisive is about to take place"—"a stupendous crisis" such as this world has never seen *(Education,* p. 179). Even now the angels restraining the winds of strife seem

God, My Refuge in the Time of Trouble

to be releasing their grip (see *Testimonies*, vol. 6, p. 408). The gathering storm increases its fury with each passing day's events.

Fearful scenes transpire on every hand. Natural disasters, social upheaval, political powder kegs, and tragedies of all kinds fill our world. They confront us so persistently that we develop a kind of immunity to their true import.

Trouble is usually worse in anticipation than in reality, but in the crisis before us, "the most vivid presentation cannot reach the magnitude of the ordeal."—*The Great Controversy*, p. 622. A "time of trouble, such as never was since there was a nation" (Dan. 12:1), looms before us.

The great prophecies of Daniel and Revelation furnish chart and compass for God's people living on the very knife-edge of time. But the Psalms, like a competent pilot at the helm, provide courage and hope to the passengers on the good ship Zion.

Many of the psalms, conceived in the heat of battle or in the furnace of affliction, speak of trouble, distress, oppression, and persecution. With Saul hot on his tracks, David cried out, "Save me, O God. . . . Oppressors seek after my soul" (Ps. 54:1-3). "Deliver me from mine enemies, O my God" (Ps. 59:1). He recognized his only real protection:

"Yea, in the shadow of thy wings will I make my refuge,
until these calamities be overpast." Ps. 57:1.

Fleeing to the wilderness of Paran after the death of his trusted friend and counselor Samuel, David composed the beautiful 121st Psalm, "My Help Cometh from the Lord" (see *Patriarchs and Prophets*, p. 664).

When faced with overwhelming heathen armies, he prayed,

Let Me Tell You About My God

> "Give us help from trouble:
> for vain is the help of man." Ps. 60:11.

And when his own son led a coup against him, he sang (see *Patriarchs and Prophets*, p. 741):

> "Lord, how are they increased that trouble me!
> many are they that rise up against me. . . .
> I laid me down and slept;
> I awaked; for the Lord sustained me.
> I will not be afraid of ten thousands of people,
> that have set themselves against me round about."
> Ps. 3:1-6.

No wonder God's people in all ages have loved and cherished such songs of confidence in times of trouble. How many martyrs for Christ have breathed their last with some psalm on their lips? The Reformers of the church relied on the psalms for courage and strength in their battles.

But the lofty Mount Everest of the psalms for times of danger and trauma—Psalm 91, with its rich promises— seems especially designed to shelter in its shadow those facing the greatest crisis of all ages. Its message should be deeply etched on the memory of every child of God.

The authorship of Psalm 91 is uncertain. Some think Moses may have written it, since it follows his poem, the 90th. A number of the expressions remind us of him: "The most High," the eagle spreading her wings over her young (see Deut. 32:8, 11), and "the eternal God is thy refuge, and underneath are the everlasting arms" (chap. 33:27). Other expressions sound familiarly like the Davidic psalms. But whoever the author, the psalm, with its skillful use of images, its lively word pictures, and its fast-moving scenarios, has a universal appeal.

The shift of voices in it indicates its probable use in the temple liturgy. Beginning with a personal affirmation of trust in the Lord, it moves to promises for the hearer, and finally ends with the voice of God Himself assuring the believer of His love, His presence, and His blessing.

"THE SHELTER OF THE MOST HIGH."
"He who dwells in the shelter of the Most High
will rest in the shadow of the Almighty." Ps. 91:1,
N.I.V.

Every living creature needs shelter. From the tiniest little spider seeking to find a home in the corner of your room to man, all seek a safe hiding place. The more secret, the safer in times of danger. The little house wren or the friendly robin often builds its nest near human habitations, the oriole usually finds safety high in some tree, while the meadowlark or song sparrow hides its ground nest with grass and weeds. But all desire shelter and protection from danger and predators for themselves and their young. Shelter means security. And security brings rest.

Weiser suggests that "dwelling in the hiding-place of God is meant to express the safety and peace of mind that come from a sense of protection against persecution, whereas staying overnight in the shadow of the Almighty is meant to express that feeling of being out of danger which springs from the knowledge that someone else keeps guard."—*The Psalms: A Commentary*, p. 606.

No matter how great the danger, how deep the distress, how threatening the enemy, the child of God—hiding in the secret place of the Most High, knowing He keeps guard—can say with the psalmist:

"I will both lay me down in peace, and sleep:
for thou, Lord, only makest me dwell in safety." Ps.
4:8.

The search for safety today is epidemic. Some build underground shelters. Most imprison themselves behind safety locks and chains. Still others flee the crowded urban jungles for the suburbs, and the more fortunate ones obtain some remote country dwelling.

But according to the psalmist, the most unlikely place may be the safest:

"He shall cover thee with his feathers,
and under his wings shalt thou trust." Ps. 91:4.

Birds of all sizes use their wings to insulate their young from the elements and protect them from predators. The eagle, with a wingspread of seven feet or more, protects its young in the nest with its mighty wings. The wings of the Almighty are both large enough and strong enough to shelter all who desire to place their trust there.

"If you live in the shelter of Elyon
and make your home in the shadow of Shaddai,
you can say to Yahweh, 'My refuge, my fortress,
my God in whom I trust!'" Verses 1, 2, Jerusalem.

The psalmist uses four divine names close together. *"Most High* is a title that cuts every threat down to size; *Almighty* (Shaddai) is the name that sustained the homeless patriarchs (Ex. 6:3). . . . *The Lord* (Yahweh) . . . [assures] that 'I am' and 'I am with you' (Ex. 3:14, 12, N.E.B.); . . . *God* is made intimate by the possessive, as *my God."*—D. Kidner, *Psalms 73-150: An Introduction and Commentary,* p. 332.

Sanford T. Whitman tells of visiting one of his parishioners who lived high up in a mountain wilderness hideaway. Admiring the magnificent scenery, he couldn't help wondering what it was like in the winter. "Aren't you afraid of being snowed in?"

With a smile of amusement the mountaineer explained happily, "Naw, gettin' snowed in ain't the problem. We always make sure we're ready for that. *Gettin' snowed out is what we wish would never happen."* And in those few short sentences, Whitman said, "this man had preached one of the great sermons of the gospel."—*Signs of the Times*, December, 1981, p. 16.

Suppose that when the storm of last-day trouble comes, we find ourselves stranded far from home and shelter, with the roads blocked by snowdrifts of impossibility? But with our lives hid in God, what matter if the storm rages, the tempest blows, or the enemy attacks? Safely protected in Him, "the rock that is higher than I" (Ps. 61:3), we can say with the psalmist:

"For thou hast been a shelter for me,
and a strong tower from the enemy." Verse 3.

"Come my people, enter thou into thy chambers, and shut thy doors about thee: hide thyself . . . until the indignation be overpast" (Isa. 26:20).

"THE SNARE OF THE FOWLER." The fowler, or bird trapper, cleverly places his traps to catch the unsuspecting victim before the creature knows what has happened to him. The same enemy who roars like a lion also appears as a beautiful enticing serpent, seeking to deceive "the very elect" (see Matt. 24:23-26). While "no man is safe for a day or an hour without prayer," yet "Satan is well aware that the weakest soul who abides in Christ is more than a match for the hosts of darkness."—*The Great Controversy*, p. 530. "Nestle in the sheltering arms of Jesus, and do not wrestle yourself out of His arms."—*This Day With God*, p. 9.

"THOU SHALT NOT BE AFRAID." The time of trouble! The very words still conjure up for me vivid and frightening childhood images of deep, dark underground torture chambers, where many of us would eventually spend our last days.

A young mother, brought up in the church, explained

to a visiting pastor that she left it because she didn't want her children to have to suffer through "the time of trouble."

A newly baptized church member approached me one day with great consternation, frightened by the terrible descriptions of the time of trouble a fellow member had been sharing with her.

A young man we know, upon hearing a discussion of "the time of trouble," went out and purchased an expensive weapon for self-protection.

Is the Biblical teaching of a time of trouble meant to frighten us to godly living? Or to give us something sensational to speculate on? Or should we downplay the whole thing and ignore it altogether? Will denial keep it from happening?

A whole segment of the Christian community does just that. It teaches that before the great tribulation of the last days God will rapture away Christians to enjoy the bliss of heaven while the remainder of the population suffers through seven terrible years under the rule of antichrist. Such teaching may appeal to the human desire to avert difficulty, but what happens to them when they find themselves facing calamities and conflict for which they failed to prepare?

And what about those who, immobilized by fear, put off preparation for the dreaded inevitable? The psalmist answers with confidence:

"Thou shalt not be afraid for the terror by night;
nor for the arrow that flieth by day;
nor for the pestilence that walketh in darkness;
nor for the destruction that wasteth at noonday."
Ps. 91:5, 6.

God, My Refuge in the Time of Trouble

Terrors will come—believers victimized by terrorist groups in many parts of the world know that all too well! God's people will be targets for the arrows of false accusation and vicious attacks. Pestilence and destruction respect no one. God never promised immunity from all trouble. But He does provide freedom from the most dreaded enemy of all—*fear!*

"I sought the Lord, and he heard me,
and *delivered me from all my fears.*" Ps. 34:4.
"What time I am afraid, I will trust in thee. . . .
I will not be afraid what man can do unto me." Ps. 56:3-11.

Spurgeon tells of coming home from a funeral during the great cholera epidemic of 1854. Discouraged and overcome by what he saw of the ravages of the disease and death on every hand, he began to fear that he himself would succumb to the plague. Walking by a shoemaker's shop in old London, his eye caught the following words hanging in the window, which refreshed and strengthened him to continue his ministry without any ill effects (*Psalms*, on Ps. 91:9, 10).

"Because thou hast made the Lord,
which is my refuge, even the most High, thy habitation;
There shall no evil befall thee,
neither shall any plague come nigh thy dwelling."
Ps. 91:9, 10.

"IT SHALL NOT COME NIGH THEE." Nothing can touch you except by His permission! Thousands may fall around you, but "it shall not come nigh thee" (verse 7).

When the three Hebrew young men faced the fiery furnace for their loyalty to the God of heaven, they made it clear to Nebuchadnezzar that whether God saw fit to deliver them or not, their faith in Him remained the same. And because the Son of God walked with them into the furnace, they escaped without even a singed hair or the smell of fire.

But this promise specifically refers to the plagues. "Neither shall any plague come nigh thy dwelling." The plagues on the Egyptians at the time of the Exodus fell as judgments against the objects of their worship. So in the last days of earth's history the plagues will fall on them "which had the mark of the beast, and . . . which worshipped his image" (Rev. 16:2).

"The Lord shall preserve thee from all evil:
    he shall preserve thy soul." Ps. 121:7.

"The people of God will not be free from suffering; but while persecuted and distressed, while they endure privation and suffer for want of food they will not be left to perish. That God who cared for Elijah will not pass by one of His self-sacrificing children. He who numbers the hairs of their head will care for them, and in time of famine they shall be satisfied."—*The Great Controversy*, p. 629; see also Isa. 33:16; 41:17.

"HE SHALL GIVE HIS ANGELS CHARGE OVER THEE." How little we know of the important and constant work of these "body guards" (as Spurgeon calls them) that keep their vigil for those "who shall be heirs of salvation" (Heb. 1:14). Because we cannot see them, and because the devil misused the promise of Psalm 91:11 in the wilderness temptation (Matt. 4:6), we fail to appreciate it as much as we should.

To those who follow Christ, "angels that excel in strength are sent from heaven to protect them. The wicked one cannot break through the guard which God has stationed about His people."—*Ibid.*, p. 517.

"The angel of the Lord encampeth round about

them that fear him, and delivereth them." Ps. 34:7.

Like Elisha's servant, we need to have our eyes opened to see that "they that be with us are more than they that be with them" (2 Kings 6:16).

"I WILL DELIVER HIM." On March 31, 1982, a huge avalanche of snow thundered down the mountain through Alpine Meadows ski resort in California, snuffing out seven lives, but miraculously sparing four others. Anna Conrad, caught in a kind of shelter formed by large wooden lockers, survived for five or six days before anyone reached her. "I'm OK. I'm alive!" she announced when the rescue team reached her. As the rescue helicopter lifted her to safety, she saw for the first time the terrible havoc of the storm—five acres of devastation almost beyond imagination (see *National Geographic*, September, 1982, pp. 282-285).

Ominous signs remind us that an avalanche of trouble is about to break upon our world. But if we have hid our lives in God, sheltered ourselves intimately under His everlasting wings, like Anna Conrad we may not know its extent and magnitude till it's all over. Like her, we may barely survive physically, but when rescue comes we too may be able to say, "I'm OK. I'm alive!"

And to His children, living in such a time, our wonderful God speaks reassuring promises that should burn their way into our innermost consciousness:

"Because he hath set his love upon me,
therefore will I deliver him:
I will be with him in trouble;
I will deliver him, and honour him.
With long life will I satisfy him,
and shew him my salvation." Ps. 91:14-16.

Chapter 12

Exalt My God the King

Let me tell you about my Saviour—the triumphant Messiah—King of the Psalms.

"The Lord reigns, . . .
he sits enthroned between the cherubim." Ps. 99:1, N.I.V.

"I will exalt you, my God the King;
I will praise your name for ever and ever." Ps. 145:1, N.I.V.

Many of the great hymns of praise in the Psalms contain profound prophetic utterances that encompass the reign of Yahweh, Israel's God, in both the first and Second Advent. Among them, the elegant coronation or royal psalms (Ps. 2, 72, 110, et cetera) provide the setting for some of the most sublime prophecies of the Messiah-King anywhere in Scripture.

To appreciate their significance, we must see them in their historical frame. Many ancient oriental cultures considered their kings as gods, their power and authority often measured by the number of vassal nations in subjection to them.

God gave Israel a king, by their demand (see 1 Sam. 8:19, 20), but with explicit instructions that he be chosen by divine will, that he not lead them away from God nor indulge himself with the extravagances of the surrounding pagan rulers (see Deut. 17:14-20), and that his authority be subordinate to divine control (1 Sam. 12:14, 15).

Most of the royal psalms, written by David at the height of Israel's power and glory as a nation—under his and Solomon's reign—reflect this ideal of the glory of a nation under God. Though that splendor gradually dimmed, and the monarchy eventually fell, the royal psalms tells us much of the great Messiah-King whom David's throne typified, and of God's ultimate purpose for His people under His rule.

THE NATIONS DEFY GOD'S ANOINTED: PSALM 2. The second psalm, frequently quoted by number in the New Testament, portrays in a few terse words the broad sweep of the great struggle between good and evil. Angry nations, defiant and rebellious (verse 2), bent on breaking from Israel's power, challenge them and their God:

"'Let us break their chains,' they say,
and throw off their fetters.'" Verse 3, N.I.V.

But it is no mere political struggle against Israel:

"Why do the nations rage
and the peoples plot in vain?
The kings of the earth take their stand
and the rulers gather together
against the Lord
and against his Anointed One." Verses 1, 2,
N.I.V.

The Hebrew word used here for "anointed" translates into our word *Messiah* (see Dan. 9:25, 26). Prophets and people looked for the coming of the Messiah as the king of Israel. Nathaniel, when he met Jesus, declared, "Rabbi, thou art the Son of God; thou art the King of Israel" (John 1:49).

The high priest at Jesus' trial demanded, "Tell us

whether thou be the Christ, the Son of God" (Matt. 26:63). A few hours later the Jewish leaders chided Pilate for the title on the cross, "Jesus of Nazareth, the King of the Jews" (John 19:19). Their objection amounted to an indirect admission that He indeed was the looked-for Messiah-King.

But though men and nations vent their rage against God and His Anointed, the psalmist envisions the behind-the-scenes reality:

"The One enthroned in heaven laughs;
the Lord scoffs at them.
Then he rebukes them in his anger
and terrifies them in his wrath." Verses 4, 5, N.I.V.

God's laughing at the puny efforts of men and nations in rebellion against Him also portends His wrath and displeasure. After their arrest and release for preaching in the Temple, Peter and John quoted Psalm 2, applying the rage of the nations against "thy holy child Jesus, whom thou hast anointed" to Herod, Pilate, the Gentiles, "and the people of Israel" (Acts 4:25-27).

The voice of God now decrees:

"'I have installed my King
on Zion, my holy hill.'" Verse 6, N.I.V.

And through the psalmist, the Son responds:

"I will proclaim the decree of the Lord:
He said to me, 'You are my Son;
today I have become your Father.'" Verse 7, N.I.V.

To Christ alone the Father declares, "Thou art my Son, this day have I begotten thee" (Heb. 1:5, quoting Ps. 2:7). The word *begotten* as used in the K.J.V. implies a relationship, rather than a literal idea of begetting. (See *Theological Wordbook of the Old Testament*, vol. 1, p. 379.) "In Christ is life, original, unborrowed, underived."—*The Desire of Ages*, p. 530.

The Father confirmed His Sonship on at least two occasions: His baptism (see Matt. 3:17) and at His resurrection. In Acts 13:33 Paul applied the passage to the resurrection, linking it with another great prophetic psalm:

"For thou wilt not leave my soul in hell;
  neither wilt thou suffer thine Holy One to see corruption." Ps. 16:10.

The resurrection of Christ, the very heart and center of the apostles' teaching and preaching, attests the living proof that He indeed was God (see Heb. 1:2, 3; *The Desire of Ages*, p. 785).

His ultimate "dominion, and glory," pictured in dramatic images, "shall not pass away" nor "be destroyed" (Dan. 7:14; cf. 2:45; Rev. 2:26, 27).

"'And I will make the nations your inheritance,
  the ends of the earth your possession.
You will rule them with an iron scepter;
  you will dash them to pieces like pottery.'"
    Verses 8, 9, N.I.V.

Many commentators see in the last few verses a fourth voice—the Holy Spirit's appeal to the nations to "be wise; be warned"; be reconciled to Him:

"Serve the Lord with fear. . . .
  Kiss the Son, lest he be angry
  and you be destroyed in your way,
  for his wrath can flare up in a moment.
  Blessed are all who take refuge in him."
    Verses 11, 12, N.I.V.

To serve Him means to pay homage to Him, and to kiss Him means to be reconciled to Him. When He comes as King of kings and Lord of lords, all who do not have a restored relationship with Him will "perish" (see John 3:16, 18). But "every knee should bow . . . and every tongue . . . confess that Jesus Christ is Lord" (Phil. 2:10, 11). For some that acknowledgment will come too late (see Rev. 16:1). "There is no *refuge* from Him: only *in Him*."—D. Kidner, *Psalms 1-72: An Introduction and Commentary*, p. 53.

✓ THE REJECTED STONE: PSALM 118:22, 23. We make the choice for or against Christ. Pilate did—and it haunted him the rest of his life. Judas did—and brought disgrace and infamy on his own head. The priests and leaders of Christ's day did—"He came unto His own, and his own received him not" (John 1:11).

Jesus appealed to them to see the truth of His identity in the parable of the vineyard and the husbandmen. But they pronounced their own doom on themselves (see Matt. 21:41). He then quoted a familiar psalm, which they had often applied to the coming Messiah (verses 42, 44):

"The stone which the builders refused
is become the head stone of the corner.
This is the Lord's doing;
it is marvellous in our eyes." Verses 22, 23.

Now that Stone had spoken, but they had refused to hear. Today men and nations still reject the True Cornerstone, to them "a stone of stumbling, and a rock of offense" (1 Peter 2:8). "So it will be in the great final day, when judgment shall fall upon the rejecters of God's grace. Christ, their rock of offense, will then appear to them as an avenging mountain. . . . Because of love rejected, grace despised, the sinner will be destroyed."—*The Desire of Ages*, p. 600.

But to those who believe, "he is precious" (1 Peter 2:7). Saul of Tarsus opposed Him, dodged Him, and persecuted His followers, until one day he encountered Him on the Damascus Road. After that he considered everything as "rubbish" compared to the "surpassing greatness of knowing Jesus Christ" (Phil. 3:7, 8, N.I.V.).

Ken had rarely seen the inside of a church before his twentieth birthday. (Fortunately, his mother had instilled in him a love for spiritual things.) But on that day he vowed to seek out an Adventist church on the first Sabbath of the new year. A Minnesota blizzard, a -20° F. temperature, and a balking car could not dissuade him from his new commitment that Sabbath morning. A voice seemed to say to him, "If you don't do it today, you may never do it." The Lord has been precious to him ever since. (And both to me, for I carry both their names.)

"Today if ye will hear his voice,
    harden not your heart." Ps. 95:7, 8.

THE KING RECEIVES HIS DOMINION: PSALM 110. The New Testament quotes this pearl of the Messianic songs more frequently than any other. Its every line breathes of Messiah's reign. David portrays One greater than himself, Yahweh the Father, saying to His Son, David's Lord:

"The Lord says to my Lord:
'Sit at my right hand
until I make your enemies
a footstool for your feet.'" Verse 1, N.I.V.

By the time of Christ the Jews understood it as a clear reference to the Messianic reign. They also believed that the Christ would be of the lineage of David. Once Jesus pointedly asked His opponents, "What think ye of Christ? whose son is he? They say unto him, The Son of David. He saith unto them, How then doth David in spirit call him Lord, saying, The Lord said unto my Lord, Sit thou on my right hand, till I make thine enemies thy footstool? If David then call him Lord, how is he his son?" (Matt. 22:42-45).

Peter and John on the day of Pentecost relied on such psalms to substantiate their teaching of Jesus as the true Messiah of Israel. Reminding them that "the patriarch David . . . is both dead and buried" and that the One to be raised up to sit on his throne had come, they proclaimed, "Therefore being by the right hand of God exalted, and having received of the Father the promise of the Holy Ghost, he hath shed forth this, which ye now see and hear. For David is not ascended into the heavens: but he saith himself, The Lord said unto my Lord, Sit thou on my right hand. . . . Therefore let all the house of Israel know assuredly, that God hath made that same Jesus whom ye have crucified, both Lord and Christ" (Acts 2:33-36).

"God exalted Him as emphatically as man rejected Him."—D. Kidner, *Psalms 73-150: An Introduction and Commentary*, p. 393. "Arrayed in holy majesty" (Ps. 110:3, N.I.V.), He sits on the Father's right hand (see Acts 5:30; Heb. 1:13) and rules over His enemies (Ps. 110:2).

Then the psalmist depicts yet another phase of His reign:

"The Lord has sworn
and will not change his mind:
'You are a priest forever,
in the order of Melchizedek.'" Verse 4, N.I.V.

The author of Hebrews quotes the prophecy in applying the priesthood to Christ (Heb. 7:17). He reigns as Priest-King. "We have such an high priest, who is set on the right hand of the throne of the Majesty in the heavens; a minister of the sanctuary, and of the true tabernacle, which the Lord pitched, and not man" (Heb. 8:1, 2). "In Christ the priesthood and the kingship are united as they were in Melchizedek, the king of Salem, priest of God."—*The SDA Bible Commentary*, on Ps. 110:4, p. 880.

Jesus' position as Priest-King, which He serves as in the heavenly sanctuary, presents the Messiah's greatest triumph in the cosmic struggle between Christ and Satan for the dominion of the earth and its inhabitants. His death on the cross earned Him the right to justify them, to "save completely" (Heb. 7:25, N.I.V.). "It is His *royal right* to save unto the uttermost all who come unto God by Him."—*The Desire of Ages,* p. 751. (Italics supplied.)

Psalm 110 ends with a picture of the Lord striking "through kings in the day of his wrath" (verse 5). Though His final triumph over His enemies is yet future, the way has been opened for all who will be "willing in the day of thy power" (verse 3) to be victorious through Him. His work as Priest-King continues. The battle for the dominion rages, but His "crushing the rulers of the whole earth" (verse 6, N.I.V.) has been made certain.

Knowing the outcome, knowing our Priest-King, we can be refreshed and encouraged with Him by a "drink of the brook in the way" (verse 7).

HIS RIGHTEOUS RULE: PSALM 72. Probably written by David for Solomon, the psalm pictures an idyllic reign that neither David nor Solomon, nor any of their posterity, ever reached. Rather, it radiantly portrays the glorious reign of the Messiah-King. He will govern with righteousness and equity (verses 2-4). His rulership will be marked with peace and prosperity (verses 6, 7) and His domain will be universal (verses 8, 19) and eternal (verse 17). All will worship Him (verse 11). His praise will be the daily theme of His subjects (verse 15).

"Praise be to his glorious name forever;
    may the whole earth be filled with his glory."
    Verse 19, N.I.V.
"THE KING OF GLORY": PSALM 24. Psalm 24,

131

written for the occasion of David's transfer of the ark to Mount Zion, begins with an affirmation of God's creatorship, and a recital of the entrance requirements for worship in the temple. Imagine two choirs singing the psalm responsively as the ark passed through the gates of the city in a grand processional (see 2 Samuel 6 and 1 Chronicles 15). Handel's *Messiah* effectively interprets the antiphonal nature of verses 7-10 in the chorus "Lift Up Your Heads, O Ye Gates."

The scene changes. Listen now as the angelic choirs present this great inaugural anthem at Christ's ascension. Joyful anticipation fills the heavenly hosts as they await the return of their loved Commander after thirty-three earthly years of absence. Standing in perfect formation, ready to burst into music, the heavenly choir hears the King's approaching escort proclaim:

"Gates, raise your arches,

rise, you ancient doors,

let the king of glory in!" Verse 7, Jerusalem.

Back comes the question from the choir of adoring angels, who delight to hear His praises:

"Who is this king of glory?

Yahweh the strong, the valiant,

Yahweh valiant in battle!" Verse 8, Jerusalem.

The gates swing open wide, and amid bursts of rapturous song, they escort the King into the presence of the Father, who awaits Him with open arms. Having conquered the foe, He presents the first fruits of His victory to the Father as a token of the final great triumph yet to come.

Today Jim called and wept over the phone because his young life has seemingly fallen apart. "Why doesn't the Lord put an end to all this sin and suffering?" he cried in anger and frustration.

"Because of you and me, Jim," I answered. "If He

Exalt My God the King

came today we might not be ready. And before the triumph can be complete, the 'Lord of Hosts, mighty in battle' must meet the wily foe and ovecome him in your heart and life, Jim, and in mine!'"

Satan, a conquered foe, knows he has but a short time (Rev. 12:12). Now, like a roaring lion, he works havoc and seeks to destroy. But one day soon he will be a vanquished foe!

SONGS OF TRIUMPH: PSALMS 149, 150. The Hallel psalms (Psalms 146-150) celebrate the grand triumph of the great King with songs of exalted praise. Each of them begins and ends with "Hallelujah!" (translated "Praise ye the Lord" in the K.J.V.). The Greek transliteration—alleluia—appears four times in Revelation 19 in John's description of Christ's final victory, but is found nowhere else in the New Testament.

The revelator, as he beheld some of the thrilling scenes of the last contest between Christ and Satan, echoed the majestic notes of praise found in these psalms:

"I heard a great voice of much people in heaven, saying, Alleluia;

Salvation, and glory, and honour, and power, unto the Lord our God." Rev. 19:1.

John saw Jesus riding forth on a white horse, symbol of royalty and military might, His vesture dipped in blood—the high cost of the victory—and on it "a name written: KING OF KINGS, AND LORD OF LORDS" (verses 11, 13, 16). His eyes, flames of fire, penetrated the thoughts and secrets of every heart (verse 12). The "Faithful and True . . . doth judge and make war" (verse 11).

The armies of heaven, clothed in white, follow the triumphant King, whose "twoedged Sword" (Ps. 149:6) smites the nations who for so long have opposed Him. Now "he shall rule them with a rod of iron: and he treadeth the winepress of the fierceness and wrath of Almighty God" (Rev. 19:15; see Ps. 149:7, 8).

The marriage supper of the Lamb has come. Those called have made themselves ready, "arrayed in fine linen, clean and white" (Rev. 19:7-9). They sing a new song (chap. 14:3):

"Alleluia!

Sing Yahweh a new song,

let the congregation of the faithful sing his praise!

Let Israel rejoice in his Maker,

and Zion's children exult in their King." Ps. 149:1, 2, Jerusalem.

A voice from the throne proclaims:

"Praise our God, all ye his servants,

and ye that fear him, both small and great." Rev. 19:5.

Then a great antiphonal choir responds, perhaps accompanied by the celestial orchestra of heaven, "the voice of a great multitude, and as the voice of many waters, and . . . thunderings, saying,

"Alleluia:

for the Lord God omnipotent reigneth.

Let us be glad and rejoice,

and give honour to him:

for the marriage of the Lamb is come,

and his wife hath made herself ready." Verses 6, 7.

The Psalter closes with a doxology—a universal call to praise our wonderful God and King, in celebration of His accomplishments and His majestic greatness:

"Alleluia!

Praise God in his Temple on earth,

praise him in his temple in heaven,

praise him for his mighty achievements,

Exalt My God the King

praise him for his transcendent greatness! . . .
Let everything that breathes praise Yahweh!

Alleluia!

Ps. 150:1-6, Jerusalem.

Chapter 13

Zion,
City of the Great King

> Let me tell you about my God, the great King of Zion.
> "The Lord is great in Zion." Ps. 99:2.
> "Let the children of Zion
> be joyful in their King." Ps. 149:2.
> "Praise thy God, O Zion." Ps. 147:12.

REMEMBER ZION. Hard times had come upon God's people. Exiles in a strange land, far from their beloved Jerusalem, they sat "by the rivers of Babylon" weeping (Ps. 137:1-3). The older folk nostalgically recalled bygone years when they had journeyed toward Jerusalem for the Feast of Tabernacles. Joyfully singing the songs of Zion as they fellowshiped together, anticipating the first sight of the Temple at Jerusalem, all had made the occasion the highlight of the year.

But now, with their harps hung on willow trees to express their deep sorrow, they listened to the mockery and ridicule of their captors:

"Sing us one of the songs of Zion." Ps. 137:3.

To the cruel taunt they responded:

"How shall we sing the Lord's song in a strange land?" Verse 4.

Then in spite of the derision, in spite of their homesickness for Jerusalem, the captives remember Zion. Prophecies of its future prosperity spur them on and fan the flicker of hope in their hearts (see verses 5, 6).

"Thou shalt arise, and have mercy upon Zion:
  for the time to favour her, yea, the set time, is
    come. . . .
When the Lord shall build up Zion,
  he shall appear in his glory." Ps. 102:13-16.

Why did the word *Zion* evoke such poignant responses, such burning patriotism? What made the Zion of Scripture the pivot of Israel's worship and religious life? Why has it captured the imagination of both Jews and Christians through the centuries? What significance does it have for Christians in the last days? And what about the songs of Zion? Is anybody singing them?

HISTORY AND GEOGRAPHY OF ZION. Soon after David's coronation as king over all Israel he determined to capture the city of Jebus from the Jebusites, who had occupied the seemingly impregnable fortress off and on since the days of Joshua. Joab succeeded in conquering the stronghold for David, who made him commander in chief of his army as a result, and it consequently became David's capital (2 Sam. 5:7). Situated south of Mount Moriah, where centuries before Abraham had offered Isaac, and flanked on two sides by two deep valleys—the Kidron and Tyropoeon—the fortified mound eventually acquired the title of Mount Zion or the City of David. (Some scholars suggest that the word *Zion* may be related to an Arabic root that means "to protect" or "to defend," thus a fortress or place of defense. See *Theological Wordbook of the Old Testament*, vol. 2, p. 764.)

Eight hundred years before David's coronation, Abraham paid tithes to Melchizedek, king of Salem (from which Jerusalem gets its name), who resided in the village that would someday grow into the future metropolis of the kingdom (see *Patriarchs and Prophets*, p. 703).

When King David brought the ark of the covenant to his city, he intended to build a magnificent temple for his God. (Through his reign the sanctuary, except for the ark, remained at Gibeah. See *Patriarchs and Prophets*, p. 711.) However, God granted that privilege to his son Solomon, who built the Temple just north of David's original Mount Zion, on Mount Moriah. The Temple site consequently became known as Mount Zion, until four centuries later when the Babylonians destroyed Solomon's beautiful edifice.

In the days of Christ "a Roman ruler sat in the palace upon Mount Zion."—*The Desire of Ages*, p. 103. Christ chose for the site of His ascension, not Mount Zion, but the Mount of Olives (see *The Desire of Ages*, p. 829), which according to Zechariah 14:4 will be the site for the New Jerusalem (see also Rev. 20:9; 21:2). Apparently, then, Zion's significance does not rest on a specific geographical location.

"The crucial distinguishing factor between mythical ideas and the biblical expressions concerning Zion resides in the fact that Zion was not set apart as holy at creation. It possesses no intrinsic holiness. It became important to the Lord and to Israel only within history."—*Theological Wordbook of the Old Testament*, vol. 2, p. 764.

To understand the meaning and significance of Zion, we must see it as the Bible writers used the word. The name Zion (or Sion) occurs in 162 passages. The Psalms contain thirty-eight of them (only seven references occur before the book of Psalms). Isaiah has forty-seven texts that speak of Zion, more than in any other book. Jeremiah and his Lamentations include more than thirty passages, and thirty verses in the minor prophets mention Zion. But the Psalms set forth more clearly than any other book the theology of Zion—the reasons why God favored it.

"THE LORD HATH CHOSEN ZION."

"For the Lord has chosen Zion,
he has desired it for his dwelling:
'This is my resting place for ever and ever;
here I will sit enthroned, for I have desired it.'"
Ps. 132:13, 14, N.I.V.

God selected Abraham and called him to become father of His chosen people. He summoned Moses to lead them out of Egyptian bondage, and designated David as king and progenitor of the promised seed. And—

"He chose the tribe of Judah,
Mount Zion, which he loved." Ps. 78:68, N.I.V.

Zion was great simply because God chose it as His dwelling place!

"In Judah is God known:
his name is great in Israel.
In Salem also is his tabernacle,
and his dwelling place in Zion." Ps. 76:1, 2.

God had appeared to Solomon in a dream and promised that His presence—His eyes and heart—would be in His Temple perpetually (2 Chron. 7:16). The Shekinah glory above the mercy seat (see Ex. 25:21, 22), "the visible pavilion of Jehovah" (*The SDA Bible Commentary*, Ellen G. White Comments, on Isa. 6:1-8, p. 1139), made Zion special.

When the Philistines captured the ark in the days of Samuel, Eli's daughter-in-law gave birth to a son just as the tragic news arrived. In her dying breath she declared that the family should call her son Ichabod, "the glory is departed from Israel" (1 Sam. 4:21, 22).

At the laying of the foundation of the second Temple during the time of Ezra, some of the older men, who still remembered Solomon's Temple, wept because of the departed Shekinah glory (see Ezra 3:12). Yet Haggai the prophet predicted that the glory of the second Temple

Let Me Tell You About My God

would exceed that of the first (Haggai 2:3, 9; cf. Col. 2:9; 1
Tim. 3:16). "In the presence of Christ, and in this only,
did the second temple exceed the first in glory."—*The
Great Controversy*, p. 24 (see also Isa. 40:9; Ps. 110:2).

"Sing praises to the Lord,
which dwelleth in Zion:
declare among the people his doings."
Ps. 9:11.

Zion represented the sanctuary as the dwelling place
of God and as the center of His great acts in behalf of His
people:

"Remember thy congregation,
which thou hast purchased of old;
the rod of thine inheritance,
which thou hast redeemed;
this mount Zion, wherein thou hast dwelt." Ps.
74:2.

The saving strength of His right hand resided in the
sanctuary (Ps. 20:6) and might be implored to—

"Send thee help from the sanctuary,
and strengthen thee out of Zion." Ps. 20:2.
"For God will save Zion." Ps. 69:35.

Through the prophet Isaiah, God declared, "I will place
salvation in Zion for Israel" (Isa. 46:13; cf. chaps. 59:20;
62:11).

God also executes His judgments from Zion (see Ps.
50:2-4), especially on the "sinners in Zion" (Isa. 33:14; see
chaps. 34:8; 3:16, 17). Many of the prophets warned
against the false security of trusting in Zion while ignoring
or denying the very One who made it special (see Jer.
7:1-15; 26:1-6). And true Zion will rejoice when God
finally makes manifest His judgments:

"Zion heard, and was glad;
and the daughters of Judah rejoiced
because of thy judgments, O Lord." Ps. 97:8.

"THE LORD LOVETH . . . ZION": PSALM 87. While Zion refers specifically to the sanctuary as the dwelling place of God, the term frequently identifies Jerusalem as the holy city where God dwells (see Ps. 102:21; 128:5; 135:21; Isa,. 60:14). (Jerusalem today is anything but a holy city by the Biblical definition. For a short history of the ancient city, see *SDA Bible Dictionary*, pp. 554-564.)

The term Zion often designates God's people, the congregation (as in Ps. 74:2), thus, His church. "Say unto Zion, Thou art my people" (Isa. 51:16). The writer of the Hebrews picks up this thread, applying it especially to the New Testament church (in one of the seven New Testament texts that speak of Zion): "But ye are come unto mount Sion, and unto the city of the living God, . . . to the general assembly and church of the firstborn" (Heb. 12:22, 23).

"His foundation is in the holy mountains." Ps. 87:1. The prophet Isaiah enlarges on this idea, which became a pillar of New Testament theology (cf. 1 Peter 2:6):

"Behold, I lay in Zion for a foundation
a stone, a tried stone, a precious corner stone,
a sure foundaton." Isa. 28:16.

Those born into Zion through that precious Stone, Jesus Christ, enjoy the special privileges of the Most High Himself (Ps. 87:5).

"The Lord shall count, when he writeth up the people,
that this man was born there." Verse 6.

People of all nations and races may be proud to claim Zion as their mother (see v. 4). If you have been born in Zion (see John 3:5), your physical birthplace—in Booneville, Iowa, in Cuzco, Peru, or in Windhoek, Namibia—does not matter.

"The Lord loveth the gates of Zion

more than all the dwellings of Jacob." Verse 2.

In ancient times business matters and legal transactions often took place at a city's gates (see Amos 5:15). As in our vernacular we speak of the White House when referring to the government in Washington, so the city gates represented the institution or the organization. God loves not only the people in Zion but the body of His church!

We once had a member in one of our congregations who looked forward to the time when all the ministry of the church (his concept of the church's organization) would be jailed so the laity could hold the reins. But every part and function of the body is precious to God (1 Cor. 12:14-30).

"The church is God's fortress, His city of refuge, which He holds in a revolted world. Any betrayal of the church is treachery to Him. . . . Enfeebled and defective as it may appear, the church is the one object upon which God bestows in a special sense His supreme regard."—*The Acts of the Apostles,* pp. 11, 12.

The Lord loves the gates of Zion because His people are there. And they love Zion because He is there! And what we love we sing about.

THE PILGRIM SONGS: PSALMS 120-134. Each year the people of Israel traveled to Jerusalem for the great feasts. The songs of ascent (Psalms 120-134)—probably folk songs—celebrated the joyous occasions. They were times for sharing, for remembering their history, and for spiritual renewal.

In a few days from this writing, modern pilgrims from all over the State of Michigan will converge on the little community of Grand Ledge for an old-fashioned Adventist camp meeting. Some, like my friend Betty, have skimped and scraped for weeks to have enough money for gas to get there. Betty eagerly looks forward to camp meeting all year long for the spiritual recharging she needs as a busy wife and mother. It's an opportunity for her and for all the rest of us to remind ourselves that indeed we are modern-day pilgrims "marching upward to Zion, The beautiful city of God."

As the ancient pilgrims approached Jerusalem, they suddenly spotted the rim of Mount Zion. The Temple with its light-beige stone shone in dazzling splendor. A shout rises from the travelers. In anticipation of their goal, they sing as though they had already arrived:

"Our feet are standing
   in your gates, O Jerusalem." Ps. 122:2, N.I.V.
Admiring the beauty and order of its majestic buildings, giving the appearance of a well-planned unit, they sing:

"Jerusalem is built like a city
   that is closely compacted together." Verse 3, N.I.V.
Psalm 133 proclaims further of that unity in human fellowship:

"Behold, how good and how pleasant it is
   for brethren to dwell together in unity!" Ps. 133:1.

Psalms 122, 134, and 135 declare the joy and blessing that came in worshiping at Zion in the sanctuary.

Years of captivity often brought God's people to their knees. Looking back to other deliverances, the 126th Psalm contains a fervent prayer for God to again break their bondage, and a promise that the remnant who sow in tears will have a harvest of rejoicing (Ps. 126:4-6; cf. Ezra 9; Dan. 9:3-9; Ps. 53:6).

Psalms 121 and 125 reminded the pilgrims that their only safety came from the Lord:

"They that trust in the Lord
   shall be as mount Zion,
   which cannot be removed, but abideth for ever.
As the mountains are round about Jerusalem,

so the Lord is round about his people . . . for ever."
Ps. 125:1, 2.

"A MIGHTY FORTRESS": PSALM 46. This theme permeates Psalm 46, one of the great Zion psalms (though the word Zion does not appear in it, the references to the City of God (verse 4) and God's presence in her midst (verse 5) make it self-evident).

"God is our refuge and strength,
   a very present help in trouble." Verse 1.

The psalm inspired Martin Luther's great battle hymn of the Reformation, *"Ein' Feste Burg,"* "A Mighty Fortress."

The enemies of Zion may rage against her, they make war and seemingly overturn the earth to destroy her, but—

"God is within her, she will not fall." Verse 5, N.I.V.
"Therefore we will not fear, though the earth give way
   and the mountains fall into the heart of the sea,
   though its waters roar and foam
   and the mountains quake with their surging."
      Verses 2, 3, N.I.V.

Waves of doubt and skepticism may at times appear to swamp God's church today. Surging billows of opposition to her purpose and mission, and attacks on her foundation pillars, may beat hard against her. But the darkest hour of her struggle against the powers of evil "immediately precedes the day of her final deliverance" (*Prophets and Kings*, p. 725). As long as she remains loyal to God, "there will dwell within her the excellency of divine power" (*ibid*., p. 259). "Clad in the armor of Christ's righteousness," "there is no power that can stand against her" (*ibid*., pp. 725, 260).

The God of Jacob, the Lord of the hosts of heaven, her

Refuge (verse 11), reigns, therefore she may—
"Be still, and know that I am God." Verse 10.

"THE CITY OF THE GREAT KING": PSALM 48.
"Great is the Lord, and most worthy of praise,
in the city of our God, his holy mountain. . . .
God is in her citadels;
he has shown himself to be her fortress." Verses
1-3, N.I.V.

Zion will triumph! Not because a place called Zion is holy, nor because her people are infallible, but because of her great King. This psalm, like a brilliant diamond, reflects and at the same time brings together all the beauty, hope, and promises inherent in that word *Zion*.

"Beautiful for situation, the joy of the whole earth,
is mount Zion, on the sides of the north,
the city of the great King." Verse 2.

"Beautiful for situation." Whether the Shekinah presence above the ark, or Solomon's glorious Temple, or Immanuel, "God with us"—whether God's church then or now—Zion is "beautiful in its loftiness" (verse 2, N.I.V.). But all these meanings blend into the ultimate restoration of all things, when Mount Zion shall become "the joy of the whole earth." The expression in the K.J.V., "sides of the north," a poetic term among Israel and her neighbors, referred to the dwelling of the gods. "The city of the great King" (Verse 2) foreshadowed what the New Testament described as "The heavenly Jerusalem" (Heb. 12:22). And John the revelator heard a great voice out of heaven saying,

"and God himself shall be with them, and be their
God." Rev. 21:3.

"Behold, the tabernacle of God is with men,
and he will dwell with them, and they shall be his
people,

and God himself shall be with them, and be their God." Rev. 21:3.

Psalm 48 closes with an invitation to examine Zion: "Walk about Zion, go around her,
count her towers,
consider well her ramparts,
view her citadels." Verses 12, 13, N.I.V.

The revelator must have watched breathlessly as the view of the "great city, the holy Jerusalem" passed before him, and the angel measured the walls and the gates, revealing its dazzling splendor (Rev. 21:10-21).

Again, the revelator, standing on Mount Zion with the 144,000, listened with holy rapture to a great choir like the "voice of many waters" as they "sung . . . a new song," the song of Zion, the song of the Redeemed (chap. 14:1-3). A song of praise to the great King of Zion:
"The Lord reigneth;
let the people tremble. . . .
The Lord is great in Zion;
and he is high above all the people. . . .
Exalt the Lord our God,
and worship at his holy hill;
for the Lord our God is holy." Ps. 99:1-9.

Chapter 14

Worship Him!

Let me tell you about my wonderful God—pre-eminently worthy is He of adoration, praise, and worship.

"O worship the Lord in the beauty of holiness:
Fear before him, all the earth." Ps. 96:9.

God's last message calls on earth's inhabitants to worship the Creator (Rev. 14:7). The final great battle in the conflict between good and evil will be waged over the issue of worship (see chap 13:12, 15). Not *whether* to worship, but *whom* to worship! And whom we worship then depends on *if* and *how* we enter into the worship of the Creator *now*.

A MODERN PARABLE. Kerry Kasual spent most of his days in tacky jeans and tattered shirts that matched his life style. When asked to participate in a wedding ceremony, Kerry complied for the sake of his friend, the groom, albeit somewhat reluctantly. After enduring the several necessary hours of discomfort in a tuxedo, to no one's surprise Kerry changed back to his usual garb even before the wedding party ended.

His attitude describes the dilemma many people have toward divine worship. Realizing that their life styles are totally inappropriate for the act of worship, some shy away from it altogether, making flimsy excuses to cover the real reason. Others, perhaps to satisfy someone else's expectations, nervously put on the "tuxedo" of profession long enough to go through the ritual, but hastily return to their everyday casuals as soon as possible. Feeling uncomfortable at best, and like shams or hypocrites at the worst, they never really experience the true joy of worship. Still others go through the forms routinely, like a machine set on automatic, never giving much thought to why or how they worship.

THE PSALMS—MODELS IN WORSHIP. The Psalms express the very heart of worship in hymns of praise, intense prayers, and joyful songs of thanksgiving—all magnificently declaring the "worth-ship" of our God and Creator. Even the laments—prayers that complain, "Life is tough!" usually end on a note of praise: "But God is good!" (See R. B. Allen, *Praise! A Matter of Life and Breath*, p. 95.)

In chapter 1 we noted that the Hebrew title for the Psalter, *Tehellim*, means literally *praises*. Praise is to worship what love is to a marriage relationship, its very essence. "Praise is . . . *participation* in the worship of God. . . . Praise happens when God is glorified."—*Ibid.*, p. 73. (Italics supplied.)

True worship centers on God, not man. Too many of us when we think of worship identify it with listening to a good speaker, hearing an inspiring sermon.

Thomas K. Beecher once substituted for his popular brother, Henry Ward Beecher, at the Plymouth church in Brooklyn. When the curiosity seekers who had come to hear the famous man began to leave, Thomas raised his hand and announced: "All those who came here this morning to worship Henry Ward Beecher may now withdraw from the church; all who came to worship God may remain."—W. B. Knight, *Three Thousand Illustrations*, p. 742.

Worship Him!

Worship means more than fellowship with other believers, important as that may be to our social natures, or merely attending a service and going through certain rituals. In genuine worship we encounter the living God with a sense of awe, humility, and devotion.

I recall vividly the day that this concept of a God-encounter in worship first dawned on my consciousness. Reared in a Christian home, I had always attended church. But one Sabbath as I stood singing with the congregation in the old Keene College church, the thought intruded itself into my mind, "I wonder what it would be like to really know and love God?" That moment of awareness began for me a long and sometimes slow process of learning the meaning of true worship.

Familiarity with the forms of religion can act like tranquilizers, deadening the senses to the real meaning of worship. Yet that does not make ritual and ceremony evil, something we should automatically avoid. Throwing the baby out with the bathwater, so to speak, solves no problems. Form and order in worship please God, but He also desires the heart and soul of the worshiper.

In the Psalms we find the beautiful blending of both concepts. Ceremony and worship forms provided the vehicles for expressing the joy and excitement the psalmists found in praising the God they knew and loved. The Hebrew word *hallel* (praise Yah), transliterated "Alleluia," actually an imperative to praise, means "to be excited in joy!"

"Praise the Lord!
I will extol the Lord with all my heart
in the council of the upright and in the assembly."
Ps. 111:1, N.I.V.
"Praise the Lord, O my soul.
I will praise the Lord all my life;
I will sing praise to my God as long as I live." Ps.

146:1, 2, N.I.V.

"How good it is to sing praises to our God,
how pleasant and fitting to praise him!" Ps.
147:1, N.I.V.

A number of scholars see the praise hymns as falling into two basic types. Those of descriptive praise describe who He is and why He deserves our worship. The psalms of declarative praise proclaim His greatness revealed in His mighty acts in creation, history, redemption, and the coming judgment.

What is true worship? And how may we worship our God more acceptably?

"WORSHIP THE LORD IN THE BEAUTY OF HOLINESS." Worship is coming into the presence of the King of the universe in His house.

"Ascribe to the Lord the glory due his name;
worship the Lord in the splendor of his holiness."
Ps. 29:2, N.I.V.

To impress our minds with the greatness and reality of God's presence, the psalmist portrays the majestic and powerful voice of God in a poetic description of a storm sweeping down from Mount Hermon, across the land, into the wilderness of Kadesh.

"The God of glory thunders. . . .
The voice of the Lord is powerful;
the voice of the Lord is majestic. . . .
The voice of the Lord twists the oaks
and strips the forests bare.
And in his temple all cry, 'Glory!'" Verses 3-9, N.I.V.

The expression "beauty of holiness" (K.J.V.) or "splendor of his holiness" (N.I.V.) has created much discussion among students of the Psalms. Some translations render it as the Lord appearing in "holy array" (see R.S.V., N.A.S.B.). Artur Weiser, believing it to be what theologians term a theophany—a God-appearance—translates it: "Worship the Lord when he appears in his sanctuary!"—*The Psalms: A Commentary*. In any case, the term seems to suggest the holiness and glory of God's presence.

Moses at Mount Sinai witnessed God's presence in "thunders and lightnings" (Ex. 19:16). Upon the completion of the wilderness tent of meeting, "the glory of the Lord filled the tabernacle" (chap 40:34). Years later, when David desired to transfer the ark, the symbol of God's presence, to his city, Uzzah died for carelessly touching the sacred artifact (2 Sam. 6:7). Then the house of Obed-edom enjoyed the blessing of caring for it for a time (verses 7-12).

Solomon, after erecting a palatial building of "surpassing beauty and unrivaled splendor" (*Prophets and Kings*, p. 36), observed in his dedicatory prayer, "But will God in very deed dwell with men on the earth? behold, heaven and the heaven of heavens cannot contain thee; how much less this house which I have built!" (2 Chron. 6:18). Yet at the close of his prayer "fire came down from heaven . . . and the glory of the Lord filled the house." So great was that glory that "the priests could not enter into the house," and the people when they saw it, "bowed themselves . . . and worshipped, and praised the Lord" (chap. 7:2, 3).

The prophet Isaiah, given a vision of the "Lord sitting upon a throne, high and lifted up," his glory filling the temple, heard the voice of seraphims crying, "Holy, holy, holy, is the Lord of hosts: the whole earth is full of his glory" (Isa. 6:1-3).

Unlike the modern Christian concept, ancient Israel considered the sanctuary primarily as the dwelling place of God, and secondarily as a place of worship. The rites performed there represented God's work of salvation in behalf of the worshiper. The court where the assembly met for divine service typified the congregation's response to God's acts of salvation. The sanctuary, then, symbolized both God's presence and the worshipers' response to Him. Several of the Psalms portray this idea, but none more beautifully than the 84th:

"How lovely is your dwelling place,
O Lord Almighty!
My soul yearns, even faints
for the courts of the Lord;
my heart and my flesh cry out
for the living God." Verses 1, 2, N.I.V.

The psalmist almost envies the sparrow that has found a nest near the Lord's altar (verse 3), or the Temple officers who serve there constantly (verse 4).

"Better is one day in your courts
than a thousand elsewhere;
I would rather be a doorkeeper in the house of my God
than dwell in the tents of the wicked." Verse 10, N.I.V.

In one church we pastored we had a family recently come from Romania, who, every Sabbath morning as they entered God's house, would bow their heads in silent meditation and adoration. O that all of us might experience a keener sense of the sacredness of God's house and an awareness that the very presence of the living God dwells there!

PRAISE HIS GREAT AND AWESOME NAME. Woship is giving honor and glory to God's holy name.

"Let them praise your great and awesome name—
he is holy." Ps. 99:3, N.I.V.

"Not to us, O Lord, not to us
but to your name be the glory,

because of your love and faithfulness." Ps. 115:1,
N.I.V.

References to the name of the Lord appear nearly one
hundred times in the Psalter, with seventy-five of those
praising or extolling it. The great and eternal God
continually identifies Himself by name: Yahweh; the God
of Abraham, Isaac, and Jacob; the God of Israel; the God
of the Covenant; the God who became "flesh, and dwelt
among us" (John 1:14).

In ancient times names carried significant and often
symbolic meanings. God disclosed to Moses at the
burning bush, "I Am That I Am" (Ex. 3:14). Jesus Christ
declared, "I am the bread of life" (John 6:35). "I am the
good shepherd" (chap. 10:11).

"Holy and reverend is his name." Ps. 111:9.

How do we take His sacred name on our lips, even in
worship? "Angels, when they speak that name, veil their
faces. With what reverence, then, should we, who are
fallen and sinful, take it upon our lips!"—*Prophets and
Kings*, p. 49. Yet how often do sinful mortals use His
name carelessly, lightly, and often even in profanity.

"For they speak against thee wickedly,
and thine enemies take thy name in vain." Ps.
139:20.

Instead, let us, with the psalmist,
"Give unto the Lord the glory due unto his name."
Ps. 96:8.

"Every day I will bless thee;
and I will praise thy name for ever and ever."
Ps. 145:2.

"LET US KNEEL BEFORE THE LORD OUR
MAKER." Worship is approaching the Lord in submission, humility, and reverence.

"Come, let us bow down in worship,

let us kneel before the Lord our Maker." Ps. 95:6,
N.I.V.

Several Hebrew words express the act of obeisance in kneeling or bowing down to God or to a king. Some commentators see the word *barak,* translated "kneel" in Psalm 95:6, as being related to the word for "bless" (Ps. 145:2, K.J.V.). If blessing God means to remember, not to forget (see chapter 5 on Ps. 103: 1, 2), the act of kneeling reminds us of our submission to God.

"BRING AN OFFERING, AND COME INTO HIS COURTS." Worship is expressing our gratitude by bringing an offering to the Lord's house.

"What shall I render unto the Lord
for all his benefits toward me?" Ps. 116:12.

"I will pay my vows unto the Lord
now in the presence of all his people." Verse 14.

The Hebrew word translated as "offering" in Psalm 96:8 appears as "gift" in Psalm 45:12. The word implied the bringing of a gift as a sign of the submission and gratitude of the worshiper's total being to his Creator.

Not the size of the gift, but the giving of it, constitutes the act of worship. Jesus immortalized this principle in the story of the widow who gave her last two coins, a most insignificant contribution by monetary standards, but one of the greatest gifts of all time when measured by motive.

We sometimes hear in an offertory prayer, "Bless those who cannot give." But everyone can give something! Those few people too destitute to offer even "the widow's mites" may still present themselves.

But almost everyone, especially in the affluent societies of our world, can provide something tangible through careful planning. A little attention to our stewardship can make it possible to have something to offer the Lord every time we worship. (At our house we set aside a portion of cash each month for loose offerings, in addition to our regular tithe and contributions, so that we have something to present to the Lord at every worship service.)

"I will offer to thee the sacrifice of thanksgiving. . . .

I will pay my vows unto the Lord now

in the presence of all his people,

In the courts of the Lord's house. . . .

Praise ye the Lord." Ps. 116:17-19.

"DECLARE HIS GLORY." Worship is declaring God's praises to others.

"Proclaim his salvation day after day.

Declare his glory among the nations,

His marvelous deeds among all the peoples." Ps. 96:2, 3, N.I.V.

The public proclamation of the Word as part of worship appears throughout Scripture: "How beautiful upon the mountains are the feet of him that bringeth good tidings, . . . that publisheth salvation" (Isa. 52:7; cf. Eph. 6:15). "The Spirit of the Lord is upon me . . . to preach good tidings . . . to proclaim liberty" (Isa. 61:1, 2; cf. Luke 4:18).

An Israelite bringing his thank offering to the Temple might publicly express his gratitude. The Hebrew word *yadah*, translated "thanksgiving," suggests the idea of giving public acknowledgment or praise.

"It is good to give thanks to Yahweh, . . .

to proclaim your love at daybreak

and your faithfulness all through the night." Ps. 92:1, 2, Jerusalem.

The prophet Malachi reminds us that "they that feared the Lord spake often one to another" (Mal. 3:16). And those living under the wrath of the devil in the last days overcome him "by the word of their testimony"

(Rev. 12:11). Cherishing a sense of what our salvation has cost will motivate us to extol and magnify our Lord far more often than we do (see *Early Writings*, pp. 115, 116). The weekly prayer service, the Communion celebration—especially the ordinance of humility—along with the worship service, provide beautiful opportunities for us to declare what the Lord has done for us:

"Come and hear, all ye that fear God,
and I will declare what he hath done for my soul."
Ps. 66:16.

"I will proclaim your great deeds." Ps. 145:6, N.I.V.

Angels from the inner court of heaven listen with interest when His people assemble to worship God, for "the *testimony* of the witnesses for Christ . . . and the praise and thanksgiving from the worshipers below is taken up in the heavenly anthem" *(Testimonies*, vol. 6, p. 366; italics supplied).

"COME, LET US SING UNTO THE LORD." Worship is praising God with the voice of song and the sound of musical instruments.

"Come, let us sing for joy to the Lord;
Let us shout aloud to the Rock of our salvation.
Let us come before him with thanksgiving
and extol him with music and song." Ps. 95:1, 2,
N.I.V.

Fifteen of the psalm hymns begin with a call to or a declaration of intent to sing praises to God. Music played a vital role in the religious life of God's people, and had a far-reaching influence in freeing them from idolatry during David's reign (see *Patriarchs and Prophets*, p. 711).

Some of David's chief musicians—the sons of Asaph, Heman, and Jeduthun—exercised the prophetic office they were "set apart . . . for the ministry of prophesying," and they "prophesied, using the harp in thanking and praising the Lord" (1 Chron. 25:1, 3, N.I.V.).

Several generations later, under Jehoshaphat, king of Judah, one of Asaph's descendants, Jahaziel, also a prophet, instructed and encouraged the king and his people in the face of an invading enemy. The next day a large choir, directed by the Levites and marching at the head of Jehoshaphat's army, praised in song "the beauty of holiness" (probably with one of David's psalms) and led them to a stunning victory. (For the details of this exciting account, see 2 Chronicles 20:1-25, noting especially verse 20.)

Many psalms have served as great hymns of worship throughout the Christian era. They have inspired some of the most magnificent church music by the great composers, such as the chorales of Bach. Isaac Watts, Charles Wesley, and others wrote many of the great hymns of the Christian faith as paraphrases of psalms. Martin Luther considered music "second only to theology in the service of God."

Music, though often perverted to serve the enemy of God, when rightly employed "has wonderful power" (*Education*, p. 168). "As a part of religious service, singing is as much an act of worship as is prayer."—*Ibid*.

How important, then, that those who bear the last great call to worship the Creator plan and choose music for His worship carefully under the guidance of the Holy Spirit, and that its performance honor and glorify the One it seeks to exalt. "All the inhabitants of heaven unite in praising God. Let us learn the song of the angels now, that we may sing it when we join their shining ranks."—*Patriarchs and Prophets*, p. 289.

"Praise the Lord.

How good it is to sing praises to our God,

how pleasant and fitting to praise him!" Ps. 147:1,
N.I.V.

"LET US WORSHIP . . . THE LORD OUR
MAKER" (PSALM 95:6). Worship is the creature adoring
and magnifying the Creator.
"Know that the Lord is God.

It is he who made us, and we are his;

we are his people, the sheep of his pasture." Ps.
100:3, N.I.V.
John the revelator, peering into the throne room in
heaven, saw "four living creatures" and heard their
unceasing praises:
"'Holy, Holy, Holy

is the Lord God the Almighty,

who was, and is, and is to come.'" Rev. 4:8, N.I.V.
In response they fell down and worshiped Him and
cast their crowns before the throne, saying,
"'You are worthy, our Lord and God,

to receive glory and honor and power,

for you created all things,

and by your will they were created

and have their being.'" Verse 11, N.I.V.
Then John watched as the living creatures and the
elders prostrated themselves before the Lamb and "sang
a new song," saying,
"'You are worthy . . . ,

because you were slain,

and with your blood you pruchased men for God

from every tribe and language and people and
nation.'" Rev. 5:9, N.I.V.
"O sing unto the Lord a new song:

for he hath done marvellous things:

his right hand, and his holy arm,

have gotten him the victory." Ps. 98:1.

Worship Him!

Now the prophet listened as the celestial choir swelled the chorus:

> "'Worthy is the Lamb, who was slain,
> to receive power and wealth and wisdom and strength
> and honor and glory and praise.'" Rev. 5:12, N.I.V.

And, finally, a myriad of voices, the redeemed host, like a great antiphonal choir responded:

> "'To Him who sits on the throne and to the Lamb
> be praise and honor and glory and power,
> for ever and ever!'" Verse 13, N.I.V.

> "Praise the Lord.
> Praise the Lord from the heavens,
> Praise him in the heights above.
> Praise him, all his angels,
> Praise him, all his heavenly hosts. . . ."
> "Let them praise the name of the Lord,
> for his name alone is exalted;
> his splendor is above the earth and the heavens.
> He has raised up for his people a horn,
> the praise of all his saints,
> of Israel, the people close to his heart.
> Praise the Lord."
> Ps. 148: 1, 2, 13, 14, N.I.V.